Spirit Fire and Lightning Songs

Looking at Myth and Shamanism on a
Klamath Basin Petroglyph Site

Robert J. David

Number 66
Contributions of the Archaeological Research Facility
University of California, Berkeley

© 2016 Regents of the University of California

Published by eScholarship, Berkeley, CA

1st edition

Ebook: ISBN 978-0-9890022-2-6

Paper: ISBN 978-0-9890022-8-8

Available open access at:

www.escholarship.org/uc/item/3v65f77m

Publication of this book was made possible by funding from UC Berkeley Library and Berkeley Research Impact Initiative Funds.

Cover image: Tracing of spirit figure from 4-Mod-22 and panel photograph by Robert David. Cover design, Jerryll Moreno.

Contents

List of Illustrations	iii
Acknowledgments	v
INTRODUCTION	1
CHAPTER 1 Cultural and Environmental Setting	11
CHAPTER 2 Rock Art Recording Methods	17
CHAPTER 3 Analysis: Motifs, Markings, and Figures	25
CHAPTER 4 Interpretation of 4-Mod-22 Petroglyphs	43
CHAPTER 5 Conclusion	69
Notes	75
References	77
Index	85
About the Author	87

Illustrations

1	Panorama of 4-Mod-22	11
2	Map of Klamath Basin watershed	13
3	Map of Modoc territory	14
4	The seven entoptic forms of altered states of consciousness	20
5	The three stages of altered states of consciousness	22
6	Sample of circular figures from 4-Mod-22	26
7	Sample of skeletal figures from 4-Mod-22	27
8	Sample of anthropomorphic figures from 4-Mod-22	28
9	Sample of spirit figures from 4-Mod-22	29
10	Spirit figure engraving from Petroglyph Point	29
11	Sample of rattlesnake figures from 4-Mod-22	30
12	Coiled rattlesnake pictograph from SIS-288	31
13	Sample of triangular figures from 4-Mod-22	32
14	Stipple-traced zoomorphic Tskel figure	32
15	Stipple-traced anthropomorphic Tskel figure.	32
16	Zigzags and parallel lines covering rock face at 4-Mod-22	33
17	Example of engraved parallel lines and zigzags	34

18	Engraved lines filled with drilled holes	35
19	More examples of drilled holes	35
20	Motifs created by patterns of drilled holes	36
21	Paired zigzag figures from 4-Mod-22	37
22	Sample of grid figures from 4-Mod-22	37
23	Bisected diamond and ovoid chains from 4-Mod-22	38
24	Intersecting lines from 4-Mod-22	39
25	Plant-like figures associated with engraved zigzags	39
26	Sample of "comb" designs from 4-Mod-22	39
27	Sample of bisected lines from 4-Mod-22	40
28	Sample of barred rectangles from 4-Mod-22	40
29	Example of nucleated and concentric circles	45
30	Drilled holes associated with spirit figure from 4-Mod-22	48
31	North American pine marten	49
32	Example of Columbia Plateau "gashed" rocks	51
33	Example of California Pit and Groove Tradition engravings	52
34	Example of Klamath Basin "rain rocks"	52
35	Symbol Bridge tracing of possible tobacco plant motif	57
36	Indian tobacco	58
37	Enhanced natural fish-shaped figure	60
38	Enhanced human-like face	61
39	Half-and-half spirit figure from Columbia Plateau	63
40	Red-and-black painted bison from Altamira Cave, Spain	64
41	Split rattlesnake motif and drilled holes	64
42	Rayed sun figure on 4-Mod-22	65
43	Three anthropomorphic figures beneath elaborate zigzag	66
44	Marked pipe mouth pieces from Nightfire Island excavation	71
45	Marked pipe stem fragments	71
46	Marked bone flutes	72
47	Engraved medicinal heating stones	72

Acknowledgments

I would like to extend my deepest thanks to Anan Raymond, United States Fish and Wildlife Service Regional 6 Archaeologist, who first approached me with this project in 2007 at the Rock Art Management Symposium in Albuquerque. He not only organized the project, but with the assistance of Nicole Hurley, also carefully staked out the 10-m sections along the base of the cliff, which he used to create a detailed map of the entire rock face. I also join the rest of the crew in expressing our enthusiastic appreciation to him for arranging to house us at the Winema Lodge, whose excellent meals and hospitality provided a welcome environment in which to relax and process each day's accomplishments. Along the same lines, I am also very appreciative of the ongoing support of the Klamath Tribes Culture and Heritage Committee and to Perry Chocktoot Jr., who is the Committee's Director.

My deepest appreciation extends also to the head of the Archaeological Research Facility's (ARF) Publication Committee, Professor Christine Hastorf. Her efforts in coordinating with the reviewers and making me aware of the ARF's protocols and expectations helped me to successfully navigate the process. Thanks also to the anonymous reviewers whose thoughtful comments and critique helped to enhance the quality of this publication. While Reviewer No. 1 ensured that I understood the full range of the literature consulted for this study, Reviewer No. 2 made certain that this study was presented in a fashion that is consistent with the interests of the Klamath and Modoc people.

MaKai Magié dedicated her time, equipment, and expertise to photograph the petroglyph site with amazing attention to precision and detail. She gratefully took charge of photo documenting the site with both the GigaPan Capture and digital photography. Her patience with those of us who were less technologically savvy was very much appreciated.

Melissa Morgan assisted MaKai with the photo-documentation of the petroglyphs. She also took part in the archaeological survey where her sharp eye resulted in some impressive finds. Throughout the writing process, she also provided excellent feedback that enhanced the quality of the final report. As if that was not enough, she also came up with the monograph title. Her love, support, and intelligence will be cherished always.

Sheryl and Tom Della-Rose's participation on the survey led to the discovery and documentation of new rock art sites. Along with Sheryl's gift of the homemade chocolate chip cookies for the crew, their refreshing personalities contributed much to the project's overall enjoyment.

University of California, Berkeley, graduate Kevin Wright eagerly volunteered his energy, curiosity, and skills. In addition to his participation on the survey, he also provided much-needed assistance in documenting newly discovered petroglyph sites.

I am especially grateful to David S. Whitley, Mike W. Taylor, Jon Erlandson, and David Lewis-Williams of the Rock Art Research Institute at the University of the Witwatersrand, Johannesburg, for granting me their permission to reprint figures from their various publications.

Finally, I would like to offer special thanks to the late Dave Easly, whose ongoing passion and financial support for the preservation and study of indigenous culture through the years made this and many similar projects possible. His untimely passing will continue to leave a void in the lives of those of us he touched. It is to his memory that this publication is dedicated.

INTRODUCTION

Previous Research

In 2013 archaeologists and volunteers from Oregon and California worked together to record 4-Mod-22, a previously undocumented petroglyph site located near Tule Lake, California. The documentation was part of a larger effort by the United States Fish and Wildlife Service (USFWS) to survey and record cultural resources within an eight-hundred-acre project area on a land formation known as The Peninsula. I was contracted by the USFWS specifically because of my specialized experience in Klamath Basin rock art research and because of my Klamath-Modoc heritage. My tasks were to assist in the documentation and to write an interpretive monograph of the 4-Mod-22 petroglyphs from an indigenous perspective.

The project provided an important opportunity to follow up on the excellent work of Crotty (1981) and Lee et al. (1988) in which they studied the engravings on the more famous Petroglyph Point, also located near Tule Lake. Their studies are unique in the sense that they were among the first to view Petroglyph Point as an exclusively Modoc site rather than a mixed expression of diffused ideologies from groups outside of the region (Heizer and Clewlow Jr. 1973; Steward 1929; Swartz 1978). Turning to local ethnographic literature for insight, they explored the role vision questing and trance play in the creation of rock art. Modoc ethnography is full of references to trance-inducing rituals in which an encounter with the supernatural world was the stated goal (Ray 1963:77; Spier 1930:94–95). Within this framework they proposed that at least some of the rock art images represent "snapshots" of the supernatural world as experienced by Modoc supplicants under induced altered states of consciousness (Lee et al. 1988:136).

The recent use of Lewis-Williams and Dowson's (1988) neuropsychological model to link trance imagery in Klamath-Modoc rock art with vision questing was as innovative as it was refreshing (David 2012a:131–133; Hann and Bettles 2006:178; Loubser and Whitley 1999: 1:64–74; Whitley et al. 2004:224–227). Not only does this model help us to understand the origins of certain types of rock art, it also provides a mechanism that bridges rock art with obscure and fragmented ethnographic statements made in relation to rock art and trance. This shift in research foci has initiated a fresh and fruitful round of discussion in the Klamath Basin rock art literature. But to obtain an understanding of how some of these images functioned within the shamanic practice, and by extension, within the wider Klamath-Modoc social context, it is necessary to move forward with this model in hand and interrogate the multiple expressions of shamanic practice as a whole. Such practice might include the role of incantations, ritual smoking, ritual curing procedures, and image-making endeavors in addition to the creation of rock art, to name a few. Descriptions of these and other activities are available in Klamath-Modoc ethnographic literature, but for a more complete illustration that merges them with supernatural activities and that bridges their function with shamanic ritual, it is necessary to consult Klamath-Modoc myth.

As Lee et al. (1988:138) proposed, and as I have observed elsewhere, a more detailed understanding of rock art imagery resulting from trance is in local mythologies where the content and structure for shamanic ritual may be found (David 2010:381). For the Klamath and Modoc, myth provided the cosmological matrix through which dreams and encounters with the supernatural universe (e.g., trance) were interpreted. Through myth, trance-induced shapes acquired identity, and the random, fluid action of dreams found order that inspired and structured ritual acts (e.g., David 2010:394). In this regard, it is not possible to understand the cultural significance of Klamath-Modoc rock art without understanding its cosmological underpinnings encoded in myth. Rock art is, at its heart, a snapshot of the supernatural world as shamans experienced it through induced dream states. When taken together with ethnography and comparative imagery, myth provides a strong interpretive framework in which the meaning and purpose of 4-Mod-22 rock art might best be realized.

Previous Research

Rock art on The Peninsula first received archaeological attention by Julian Steward (1929:59–61), who affiliated it with the Great Basin Curvilinear style, which is typically associated with the hunting of big game animals. Heizer and Clewlow followed up Steward's work and began organizing the accumulated data on Californian rock art. They accepted Steward's Great Basin classification and added a Great Basin "Pecked" category as well (Heizer and Clewlow Jr. 1973:240).

In his monumental work, B. K. Swartz Jr. (1978) recorded 119 sites for the Klamath County Museum and brought this large corpus of rock art into wider academic discourse with his publication *Klamath Basin Petroglyphs*. In this study, Swartz Jr. sought to establish plausible relationships between design styles and rendering techniques of the art. Finding these categorical relationships statistically sound, he was able to comment on both the art's interpretive potential and relative chronology. Noting that the Klamath Basin was situated at a crossroads with the Columbia Plateau, the Great Basin, and the Sacramento Valley, he saw the rock art as expressions of complex interrelationships between these regions (Swartz Jr. 1978:22). Under the system of coding by Swartz Jr., site 4-Mod-22 (listed by Swartz Jr. as Tlk-4 AS-KCM) contains examples of his Complex C (Great Basin Pecked-Abstract) and Complex D (Great Basin Scratched) petroglyphs (Swartz Jr. 1978:47).

Dissatisfied with the "Great Basin" designation for the rock art of Petroglyph Point, Crotty (1981) became the first to treat this site as an exclusively Modoc creation. She correctly noted that previous studies ignored the site's environmental and cultural contexts and thus sought to relate the site's unique features to the ethnographic and archaeological records of the area. As she pointed out, Steward's characterization of Petroglyph Point petroglyphs as Great Basin types was by his own admission based on information provided to him by informants; Steward never personally visited the site (Steward 1929:53, cited in Crotty 1981:150). Yet based on his classification, Heizer and Clewlow added their Great Basin Pecked style, even though, as Crotty pointed out, the technique employed at Petroglyph Point is not pecking (Crotty 1981:153). The classification of abstract elements, in particular, raised questions about objective measurements, since there is considerable disagreement in the literature about what constitutes angular, segmented, and wavy elements. Many of these forms morph into and out of the other categories, creating "mixed" categories that have not yet been introduced into the literature. This makes comparative studies impossible (Crotty 1981:159–160). Another problem she found with the Great Basin designation is that it contributes to a history of erroneous interpretations of the site. Throughout the history of published explanations for Petroglyph Point, Modoc authorship remained in question. The perpetuation of the Great Basin style classification that Steward

(1929) offered has contributed to this dissociation by affiliating it with Shoshonean-speaking groups from the east and with big-game hunting and migration trails. But, as she pointed out, Petroglyph Point is associated with neither (Crotty 1981:164–166). Moreover, archaeological studies have shown that the cultural development of the Modoc exhibits very little influence from the Great Basin (Crotty 1981:166). Instead, taking the site's proximity to the lake and its resources into account, in addition to information derived from local ethnographies, Crotty suggested that the petroglyphs were an exclusively Modoc creation that may have been created as part of power quest rituals related to resource acquisition from the lake rather than the taking of big game (Crotty 1981:163).

Following Crotty (1981), Lee et al. (1988) examined the rock art of both Petroglyph Point and Fern Cave as exclusively Klamath-Modoc creations. They formally rejected Steward's (1929) Great Basin classification for the rock art, as well as its supposed similarity to the Santa Barbara-Tulare style, and argued instead that it represented a distinctive style all its own (Lee et al. 1988:133–135). Viewing rock art as an expression of religious belief, they joined Crotty (1981:163) in suggesting that some of the motifs may have been related to the acquisition of supernatural power (Lee et al. 1988:136). According to local ethnographies, acquiring supernatural power was achieved by inducing a state of trance through sensory deprivation and exhaustion, and the resulting dreams were intended to produce power songs (Spier 1930:95). Among the Modoc, only shamans' power quests resulted in the acquisition of these dream songs (Ray 1963:34). According to Lee et al. (1988:137) some of the imagery at Petroglyph Point may have been produced in relation to these quests. But even though stacked-rock features are a common by-product of such quests (Ray 1963:77; Spier 1930:95), they acknowledged that no stacked-rock features are located on The Peninsula. To explain their absence, they proposed that the repetition involved in making many of the Petroglyph Point carvings were analogous with the repetitive behaviors involved in power quest activities, such as rock stacking (Lee et al. 1988:137–138). In another innovative approach, they also consulted local myth to aid them in identifying other image types as well, including the medicine disk of the culture hero Kumush and a number of the "bug" motifs like the Butterfly Spirit (Lee et al. 1998:138).[1]

Loubser and Whitley (1999:1:1–2) documented eight rock art sites, all comprised largely of black-painted pictographs, within the collapsed lava tubes of Lava Beds National Monument. Acknowledging that ethnographic references to rock art are rare and often incomplete, they maintained that successful interpretations can nonetheless be achieved first by forming a general framework for interpretation through the use of wide-ranging regional ethnographic analysis and, second, by filling in the missing details with information from a particular culture or area. This is especially effective when making ethnographic analogies between culturally or linguistically related groups like the Modoc and neighboring Klamath (Loubser and Whitley 1999:1:48). Within the wider Columbia Plateau culture area, of which they consider the Klamath Basin to be a southern variant, ethnography reveals five functional explanations for rock art: shamanic vision questing; non-shamanic vision questing; hunting magic; mortuary practices; and mythological relationships (Hann et al. 2010).

Shamanic vision questing involves the ritualistic effort by shamans to acquire and use supernatural power. This was typically achieved through trance brought about by sensory deprivation, tedious labor, profuse sweating, and the use of native tobacco (*Nicotiana attenuata*). The resulting altered state of consciousness (i.e., trance) was understood to be an encounter with the spirit world, and the creation of rock art was intended to be a recording of these experiences (Loubser and Whitley 1999:1:50).

Non-shamanic vision questing involved the ritualistic acquisition and use of supernatural assistance by people who were not shamans. The reasons for this kind of quest varied but tended to center around life crises, such as the onset of puberty, death, the birth of a child, warfare, and a sustained period of serious loss from gambling. Like the shamanic quest, the goal for non-shaman supplicants was to achieve an altered state of consciousness, the experiences of which would be commemorated in the form of rock art (Loubser and Whitley 1999:1:54). The difference between this and the shamanic quest is that shamans used spirits for particular tasks, such as ritual curing or weather control, while non-shamans used them for general assistance in succeeding in challenging pursuits, such as hunting, gambling, and warfare.

Like mortuary associations, the concept of hunting magic found no expression in Klamath Basin rock art. However, other ritual specializations, such as the practice of distance killing (e.g., sorcery), is very well noted (Ray 1963:68). Distance killing was a method shamans used to eliminate their rivals by sending bad or dangerous spirits into their camps or villages. Such an event may have occurred during the Modoc War of 1872–1873 and may have involved the creation of rock art (Loubser and Whitley 1999:1:61). It was a little known fact that Captain Jack's second-in-command, Curly Headed Doctor, was a practitioner of the Ghost Dance religion. This religion professed that if Native Americans practiced the Circle Dance all Euro-Americans would disappear in a cataclysm, thus returning the land to Native American hands. Curly Headed Doctor's actions reflected this belief. Throughout the war he administered the Circle Dance himself. He made and placed a red-painted tule rope along the stronghold's perimeter, which he professed the attacking U.S. troops would never cross, and he erected a medicine pole that contained a banner of white weasel skin and hawk feathers. In relation to this, Loubser and Whitley (1999: 1:63–64) drew attention to a particular ritual intended to make the Modoc warriors impervious to bullets. Lying on the floor of Captain Jack's Cave, Curly Headed Doctor entered a frenzied trance after smoking from his medicine pipe. Loubser and Whitley suggest that this ritual may have been intended to bewitch the U.S. troops who were encamped a short distance away. Noting the strong association between trance and the creation of rock art, they proposed that some of the rock art in Jack's cave may well have been placed there by Curly Headed Doctor himself as a part of this trance.

One very strong relationship Loubser and Whitley noted was the association between Klamath Basin rock art locations and myth. The first site they pointed to is a small cave located east of Tule Lake that is actually outside of the Lava Beds National Monument. According to Hann and Bettles (2006:186) this cave was ethnographically identified as the house of Gmok'am'c the Klamath-Modoc creator deity. This cave was also a noted medicine man's cave and was believed to be an abode for spirits, making it an ideal place where people could seek out supernatural power (Riddle 1890). The second location is Petroglyph Point. As part of The Peninsula, it was the point from which Gmok'am'c created the world and all of its inhabitants. The volcanic tuft that forms this landmass is believed to be the original earth matter, which Gmok'am'c had brought up from the sacred underworld (Ray 1963:18). The third association involves the mythological being Lulusdewieas and the creation of the lava tubes within Lava Beds National Monument. In one story, following mistreatment from his daughter-in-law, Lulusdewieas painted his phallus with black pigment and then created the lava tubes by boring them out in a sort of hypersexual fashion (Curtin 1912:123). Noting that the pictographs in these cave systems are made predominantly of black pigment, Loubser and Whitley

(1999) point out that sexual symbolism is a widespread concept in far western North American ethnography that is used to express the relationship between shamans and sacred sites and, more specifically, to metaphorically refer to their encounters with the supernatural world through trance (Blackburn 1975:36; Devereux 1949:111; Gayton 1948:111; Gayton and Newman 1940:23–26; Gifford 1932:50; Kroeber 1907a:266–272; 1907b:225–227; La Barre 1980:63; Laird 1975:54, 1976:216; 1984:59; Lowie 1909:224–225; Stone 1932:55; Myers 1987 cited in Whitley 1998:19; Thrall Rogers and Gayton 1944:207).

At all three of these locations, myth provided the social and cosmological justification for their identification as sacred places and for the ritual activities with which they are associated (Loubser and Whitley 1999:1:59). The relationship between myth, rock art, and ritual practices is central to the interpretations proposed for the 4-Mod-22 petroglyphs in the current study and is discussed in greater detail in the following chapters.

Consistent throughout eight rock art sites in Loubser and Whitley's (1999) study was the predominance of trance imagery, or imagery brought about by the kinds of sensory-depriving activities characteristic of vision quest rituals. Much research has been done over the past century to understand the form, characteristics, and recurrence of the visual and sensory precepts that mammals, particularly *Homo sapiens*, experience during altered states of consciousness. By and large, this research was culminated in the neuropsychological model proposed by Lewis-Williams and Dowson, which was based largely on information gathered from human subjects under laboratory conditions, as well as cross-cultural descriptions of trances (Klüver 1926, 1942, cited in Lewis-Williams and Dowson 1988:201–202). Of particular relevance to Loubser and Whitley's (1999) study are the three stages of trance identified in this model, which I describe at length in Chapter 3.

Within each stage, subjects are drawn farther into the experience, culminating in a completely developed hallucinatory world in which they believe themselves to be an active participant (Lewis-Williams and Dowson 1988:204). Progress through these stages, though not necessarily sequential, corresponds closely with the three stages of the spirit quest procedure observed by Modoc shaman initiates (Ray 1963:31–35). Each stage of this quest was intended to draw initiates progressively deeper into the supernatural world. This experience culminated in the third and final stage in which initiates encountered particular spirit familiars and acquired the power songs that they would go on to use in their ritual practice. One notable aspect of this process relevant to Loubser and Whitley (1999) is the first phase, which was intended only to familiarize initiates with the supernatural world (Ray 1963:31–32). The forms and shapes they witnessed in their ritualized dreams (e.g., trance) during this stage appeared to them in "kaleidoscopic transition" (Ray 1963:31)—a phrase that is strongly reminiscent of the entoptic phenomena that Lewis-Williams and Dowson (1988:202) described. In fact, 87.5 percent of the motif assemblage in their study area consisted of exclusive entoptic phenomena—exactly what they expected to see if these caves had been used for the first stages of the shamans' spirit quest procedure (Loubser and Whitley 1999:1:74)!

Whitley et al. (2004) expanded on the work of Loubser and Whitley (1999) in two important ways. First, they included sites beyond the lava tubes in Lava Beds National Monument. This made it possible to test their interpretations for the lava tubes on a wider sample of sites. Second, they explored notions of Native American landscape symbolism in relation to certain patterning found throughout the North American far west. Viewing *landscape* as an active cultural agent, instrumental in harboring and even justifying Native American cosmologies, Whitley et al. (2004) reasoned that a landscape approach was highly suitable for an archaeology of religion, by which they meant the practices and beliefs that led to the production of rock art (Whitley et al. 2004:218).

In particular, they focused on three rock art site complexes on the Modoc Plateau that include the aforementioned lava tubes in Lava Beds National Monument, Petroglyph Point, and a cave referred to as Gmok'am'c's House, which is located outside of the Monument. The main tenets of this landscape symbolism model hold that rock art sites are located where supernatural power is especially concentrated on the landscape, and the rock panels bearing this art served as portals between the natural and supernatural worlds, which can be accessed by entering into an altered state of consciousness. The third aspect concerns its metaphysical underpinnings, which are culture specific. This aspect considers the relationship between the supernatural world of the shamans and mythic time-space. Among some groups, such as those in Central California and the Great Basin, for instance, these two realms formed nonintersecting sets. The shamans' source of supernatural power did not involve mythic time-space, but instead derived from a supernatural world that was contemporaneous with the natural, physical world. Myth, while still an important component of these cultures, played no role in the shamans' access to or use of supernatural power. In other regions, however, mythic time-space and the supernatural world of the shamans were entirely conflated. Supernatural power derived from the miraculous past that was inhabited by mythological beings. Shamans who attempted to tap into this power re-experienced the time-space of this mythical, magical world; mythological actors thus provided shamans with their supernatural abilities. In regions such as the Columbia Plateau, of which these authors consider the Klamath Basin to be a southern variant, this relationship is somewhat fluid, existing at various places between these extremes. This raised questions about where the Klamath Basin fits within the wider ideological framework of the North American far west (Whitley et al. 2004:223) and thus constituted a key point of their investigation.

A fundamental principle inherent in this model is the concept of symbolic inversion and how it worked to shape Native American perceptions of a spiritualized landscape. As Whitley (1998:21–23) noted, many Native American groups perceive the distribution and accessibility of supernatural power in terms of a gendered landscape. High ground was generally equated with the masculine, while low ground was equated with the feminine. Following this logic, one would expect that shamans in search of strong (masculine) supernatural power would find it in high places, such as hilltops and peaks. In fact, the opposite was true. Rock art sites in the North American far west tend to be located on low (i.e., feminine) ground. This was because of the fundamental belief in an inverted supernatural world shared by many (if not all) Native groups in western North America. In this supernatural world, everything was reversed from the natural, physical world. Day in the physical world, for instance, was night in the supernatural world, and so on. This perception carried over to the landscape as well. High (masculine) ground in the natural world translated to low (feminine) ground in the supernatural world, just as high ground in the supernatural world translated to low ground in the natural world. An excellent discussion on his topic can be found in Whitley (1998). Acting upon this logic, then, shamans understood that they could gain masculine supernatural power from low places in the natural world because this equated to a high, masculine, place in the spirit world. As a consequence, the rock art they produced is located on low ground throughout the North American far west and was one of the evaluation criteria with which Whitley et al. (2004:229) approached the sites in their Klamath Basin study.

The three site complexes in their study reflected the general tenets of Native American landscape symbolism, including the gendered landscape and the principle of inversion. Based on

Klamath-Modoc ethnographic literature and myth, they demonstrated that rock art locales were considered to be especially charged with supernatural power that was available to supplicants who approached them under vision quest conditions. Their study also revealed a strong association between rock art locales and mythical characters, places, and events, suggesting that Klamath Basin shamans derived their supernatural abilities at least in part from the world of myth. Moreover, the qualities of the landscape itself found their sacred justification from myth (Whitley et al. 2004:229–230, 232). Their analysis also revealed one site where the coincidence between rock art, ritual, and the principle of an inverted, gendered landscape departed from the expected pattern. This site is a small cave, filled with rock art, that was ethnographically identified as a shaman's cave (Riddle 1890) and reputed to be the house of the Klamath-Modoc culture hero, Gmok'am'c (Curtin 1912:7; Marriott and Rachlin 1968:44–46; Ray 1963:18). Unlike the other sites in their study, this cave is located near a mountain top. While the reason for this divergence is unclear, they proposed that it reflects a specialized function of this site within the wider shamanistic complex (Whitley et al. 2004:232–233).

     A critical distinction made by Loubser and Whitley (1999), and by Whitley et al. (2004), was the difference between shamanic and shamanistic vision questing, with a particular emphasis on the puberty quest. Shamanic vision questing simply refers to vision-questing activities carried out exclusively by shamans (Whitley et al. 2004:224). Shamanistic vision questing, by contrast, involves vision-questing activities carried out by non-shamans (Whitley et al. 2004:226). Both of these varieties, according to them, led to the production of rock art in the Klamath Basin. While this is generally supported by the wider ethnographic literature of the Columbia Plateau (Cline 1938:137–138; Hill-Tout 1978; Teit 1869, 1906:282, 1909:590, 1918, 1930:194, 282–284; York et al. 1993), as I note below, it is not supported in the local literature. Although much of the vision questing procedure for shamans was also observed by non-shaman supplicants, the manifestation of power for non-shamans came not in the form of a vision, but rather of a song they heard in a dream, which they would sing during the shamans' winter performance to demonstrate their successful acquisition of spirit help (Spier 1930:94, 112). Moreover, Klamath-Modoc ethnography has only associated rock art with shamans' activities (Dennison 1879; Gatschet 1890a:179; 1890b:149; Rau 1881:64–65; Spier 1930:142–143). In spite of the very detailed ethnographic descriptions of vision (power) quests (Spier 1930:94–95), crisis quests (Ray 1963:77–81), and puberty quests (Ray 1963:72–76; Spier 1930:68–71), the making of rock art in relation to these rites is neither mentioned nor hinted at. Given the serious consequences this would have on how we interpret the rock art of this region, it should be diligently followed up in a future study, preferably one in which new ethnographic information can be introduced that would settle the issue. Having said this, given the lack of reasonable criteria beyond (albeit strong) ethnographic analogy to go on, I proceed more cautiously than Whitley et al. (2004) in this study and do not make this assumption.

Dating Klamath Basin Rock Art

As elsewhere, dating Klamath Basin rock art is problematic for two main reasons. First, even with the advent of accelerator mass spectrometry (AMS), which requires much smaller samples than ordinary ^{14}C methods, radiocarbon dating is inherently destructive to an irreplaceable cultural resource that is considered by many to be sacred. For the Klamath and Modoc, any destruction at all is considered to be a desecration. By the same token, dating petroglyphs is still very much in its infancy, and until efficient and reliable chronometric methods are developed, only indirect or relative dating methods are likely to be employed. Yet in spite of these drawbacks, both chronometric and indirect dating efforts have been made on Lava Beds National Monument rock art sites.

Indirect Dating through Climate Models

In the first instance, Lee and Hyder (1990) examined patterns in post-Pleistocene dry cycles based on climatic and archaeological information to calculate the most likely times when the carvings of Petroglyph Point could have been made. Lee and Hyder (1990:197) noted that a wave-cut notch at 4,076 ft. amsl at Prisoner's Rock could have only been formed after Tule Lake became separated from Lake Modoc at the end of the Pleistocene. Assuming as they do that this event occurred in concert with water-level declines at other lakes in the Klamath Basin, subsequent fluctuations in the water level in Tule Lake could be observed in geological studies of other pluvial lakebeds in the northeast and east (Lee and Hyder 1990:197). In short, changing lake levels in the Fort Rock and Chewaucan basins, combined with information from Sampson's (1985) Nightfire Island study, should correspond strongly with similar changes in the water levels in Tule Lake (Lee and Hyder 1990:197). While wave action for extended periods of high water levels was expected to have cut the notches in the Petroglyph Point rock face, extended periods of low water levels were considered to be the most likely times the site would have been most accessible for making the petroglyphs (Lee and Hyder 1990:198). Because Tule Lake was a poor candidate for producing datable lake-bed terraces given the sandy soil and lava flows, they instead correlated data from the Fort Rock Lake, Chewaucan Lake, and the Klamath Basin to form a climatic model that specifically identified wet and dry trends that affected water levels in old Tule Lake (Lee and Hyder 1990:200).

Between 6400 and 5700 B.P. the lake levels would have retreated, exposing the notch at 4,076 ft. This was the earliest time the petroglyphs could have been made. An extended period of high water levels occurred again about 5000 B.P., followed by another drought around 4500 B.P., which lasted for around 2,000 years. This is the next available time that the petroglyphs could have been made (Lee and Hyder 1990:200). Finally, as Sampson's Nightfire Island study shows, high water levels at Tule Lake around 500 B.P. would have once again inundated much of the site (Sampson 1985:22). The latest petroglyphs located on the southern end of the west side of Petroglyph Point could only have been accessed from the caldera above. Yet because this area was protected from wave action, the petroglyphs would not have eroded away. Instead, many were widened and deepened through erosion, making them appear somewhat newer and less refined than other petroglyphs on the site. Lee and Hyder (1990:202) proposed that either these were much older figures (carved between 4500 and 2600 B.P.) that were not heavily eroded by the extended high water levels 500 years ago, or they were carved within the past 500 years. This has not yet been determined.

Chronometric Dating

Armitage et al. (1997:718), who dated three pictographs in Fern Cave, Lava Beds National Monument, used AMS techniques to provide the only known chronometric dates available for Klamath Basin rock art. The calibrated ages for the motifs in calendrical years are A.D. 1020–1290, 1490–1955, and 1440–1670.

Conclusions

The earliest research on Klamath Basin rock art focused largely on Petroglyph Point and, to a large extent, attempted to affiliate the designs with rock art from the Great Basin (Heizer and Clewlow 1973; Steward 1929). Beginning in the early 1980s, however, researchers started to acknowledge Klamath-Modoc authorship for these petroglyphs and sought interpretations that were grounded in local ethnographic descriptions of ritual, the most common of which was the power (vision) quest (Crotty 1981:163; Lee et al. 1988:137). Loubser and Whitley (1999:1:41) bolstered the case for trance-inspired art further by bringing Lewis-Williams and Dowson's (1988) neuropsychological model into the discussion and emphasized its effectiveness for understanding commonalities in cross-cultural descriptions of trance and rock art imagery. In the 30 or so years since its introduction into Klamath Basin literature, the trance origin of rock art has come to be widely accepted (Crotty 1981; David 2005, 2012a, 2012b; David and Morgan 2014; Hann and Bettles 2006; Hann et al. 2010; Lee et al. 1988; Loubser and Whitley 1999; Poetschat et al. 2010; Ritter 1999; Whitley et al. 2004).

As an important development within this trend, attention to the role that myth can play in rock art research has also been on the rise. These studies have ranged from the identification of specific mythological characters depicted in the rock art (Lee et al. 1988) to the complex interplay between mythological characters and events, sacred landscapes, and shamanic ritual (David 2010, 2012a, 2012b; David and Morgan 2014; Hann and Bettles 2006; Loubser and Whitley 1999; Whitley et al. 2004). In these later works, in particular, I explored myth as a structuring mechanism for shamanic ritual at a handful of Klamath Basin rock art sites. Preliminary results of these studies indicated that not only can myth help us to identify certain rock art motifs but also to understand the ritual context in which they were created. Certain mythic tales, in this sense, can be understood as a structuring guide for shamanic rituals (e.g., David 2010). This introduces the strong possibility that, by consulting myth, we can learn much about how rock art functioned in particular social contexts. As Whitley and others have noted, The Peninsula is perhaps the most sacred land formation in the Klamath-Modoc homeland (Whitley et al. 2004:231). Given the rich mythological significance associated with it, the 4-Mod-22 petroglyph site presents us with an excellent opportunity to further explore how the use of myth can help us determine the range of ritual activity expressed in the rock art at a particular site. I discuss this at length in Chapter 2.

Chapter 1

Cultural and Environmental Setting

The site 4-Mod-22 is a prehistoric petroglyph site situated along a steep volcanic cliff face of the geologic feature known as The Peninsula. The cliff extends for roughly 394 ft. (120 m) along a generally north-south volcanic (tufa) bluff overlooking the former lake bed (Figure 1). Three small rock shelters are located on the site. Two of these shelters contain petroglyphs. The first is located within section 100N100W (see Chapter 2), and the second is located in section 150N100W. The third, which contains no rock art, is located within section 160N100W. It has a smoke-blackened ceiling, and the floor is heavily littered with modern trash. Significant floor disturbance is apparent in the latter caves. Given the history of looting and vandalism in the area, it is doubtful that intact deposits have survived (Gates 1982:4). None of these caves were inspected for cultural materials during this project.

Figure 1: Panorama of site 4-Mod-22. Photo by Anan Raymond.

Petroglyphs on this site were either carved, incised, or drilled into the rock face. According to Gates (1982:4), the petroglyphs correspond with Great Basin Pecked and Great Basin Scratched categories (see Swartz Jr. 1978:17–19). A motif count was not attempted but is recommended in a future project to facilitate comparative analysis with other sites, such as Petroglyph Point. During his August 29, 1960, site visit, Swartz Jr. painted over a sample of the petroglyphs with both white and black paint in order to make them better stand out in his photographs. Gates reported on his 1982 site visit that the white paint had survived but the black had not. The white paint that Swartz Jr. applied was still present on many of the petroglyphs at the time of our August, 2013, project.

The Peninsula is the eroded remnant of a large caldera that probably formed several hundred thousand years ago when pheratomagmatic explosions of basaltic lava shot through pluvial Lake Modoc, also referred to as ancient Tule Lake (Donnelly-Nolan and Champion 1987). The caldera once extended into the southeast corner of this ancient lake, forming a peninsula comprised largely of wielded volcanic tuft. In prehistoric times, the marshes that fringed Tule Lake were particularly important, as they provided wocus and aquatic resources for the people who settled there (Ray 1963:180–184). Cattails and reeds also provided food and construction materials for clothes, baskets, shelters, and rafts. Today, the dominant vegetation found around and on top of this landform is sagebrush and European grasses (Fitzgerald 1992:4–5).

Tule Lake bears little resemblance to how it looked in late prehistoric times. Following the movement of the first white settlers into Klamath Basin, the Bureau of Reclamation drained major parts of Tule and Lower Klamath lakes and constructed a series of irrigation canals and dikes to maintain the reduced lake levels. By 1910, the former lake beds had been reduced to controlled sumps that served as wildlife refuges for migratory waterfowl. Today the water that once fed Tule and Lower Klamath lakes now provides the necessary irrigation for a variety of crops, and the lakes' capacities to support waterfowl has been drastically reduced (New Horizon Technologies 1998:3-1; Ray 1963:180–182). The Modoc, along with their northern neighbors, the Klamath, have occupied the Klamath Basin for the past 10,000 years (Cressman 1956:463; Stern 1966:4). Although they were once a unified people, they underwent a series of political separations beginning around 1780, and by the time of their earliest contact with Euro-American fur traders in 1812, they had come to settle different parts of this region (Gatschet 1890a:13). The Klamath were settled in semipermanent villages along the Klamath Marsh and Upper Klamath Lake in the north, while the Modoc had settled along the shores of Lost River and Tule Lake farther south (Figure 2). This brings up an important point regarding their political separation that must be addressed before we proceed.

Based on the date range that Lee and Hyder (1991) proposed for the Petroglyph Point petroglyphs, the petroglyphs on 4-Mod-22 were created well before the Klamath and Modoc split into two distinct groups. For that reason I frequently use the descriptor *Klamath-Modoc* in reference to any of The Peninsula's rock art sites. As was common among many North American hunter-gatherer groups, the Klamath and Modoc occupied a core homeland but tended to utilize their peripheral territories in common with neighboring groups (Jensen and Farber 1982:21–22; Spier 1930:8–10). The Modoc were divided into three geographically defined subdivisions, which, according to Ray were based largely on group consciousness and familial affiliations (Ray 1963:201). The Paskanwas, or "river people," lived in the lower Lost River Valley from the Lost River Gap to Tule Lake. The Gumbatwas lived west of a line separating Lower Klamath Lake and the Lost River, through Tule Lake, southeastward to the Modoc territorial boundary. The Kowiwas, or the "people of the far out country" lived east of this line, except for the lower valley of the Lost River ([Figure 3] Ray 1963:202–203).

Ethnography

The Klamath-Modoc economic strategy was highly formalized and dictated by the availability of food. Winter lodges were dismantled and abandoned just as soon as the local snow melted off, usually in March (Ray 1963:180). Once summer lodges were erected for those who would remain behind, the rest of the people departed to gather resources from the outer reaches of their territory. Sucker fish, salmon, and wocus seed provided their main staple foods, but they supplemented this diet with a wide variety of resources as they became available throughout the gathering season. These included elk, bear, ipos, camas root, and trout just to name a few. All throughout the gathering season runners would continually return to the summer lodges with baskets of food that would be stored for winter use. This continued until the threat of snow forced the people to return to winter villages around November to rebuild earth lodges in preparation for the approaching winter (Ray 1963:180–182; Spier 1930:145–146).

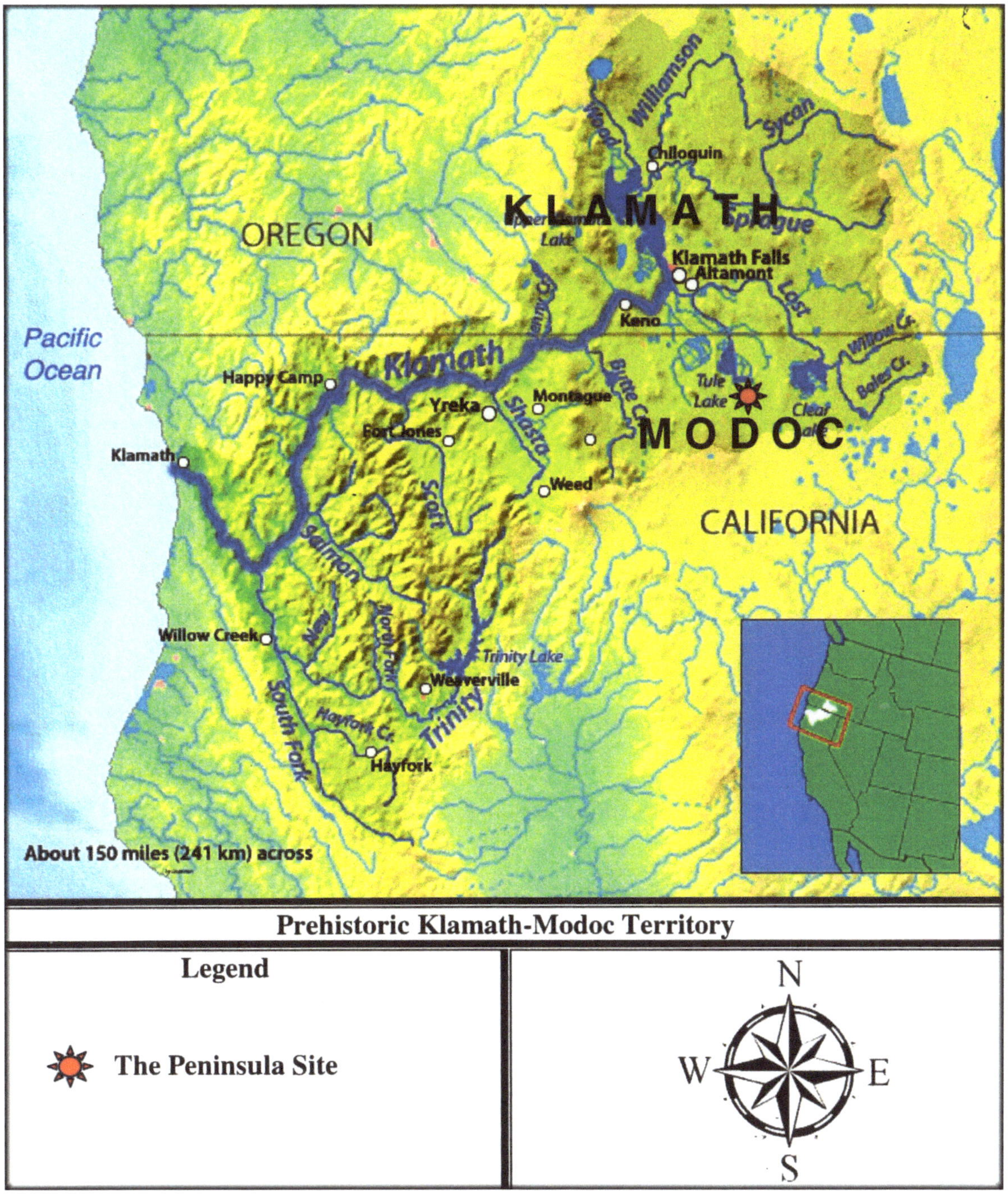

Figure 2: Map of the Klamath Basin watershed. Map by Robert David.

In spite of their political separation, the Klamath and Modoc remained culturally similar in almost all significant ways, including their use of language, their corpus of myths held in common, and their spiritual observances (Loubser and Whitley 1999:1:48; Stern 1966:4). The tenets of Klamath-Modoc religion revolved around the acquisition of supernatural power. "Everyone, perhaps without exception, seeks the powers at least once during his lifetime and further experiences seem to be repeatedly sought" (Spier 1930:94). The first of these power quests occurred at puberty. Initiates would venture into the mountains alone, fast from food and drink, and run from place to place piling rocks until spirits manifested their powers by revealing their songs in dreams (Ray 1963:33; Spier 1930:95; Stern 1966:15).² "For that reason the word for spirit is the same word used for song: *swi-is*" ([author's italics] Spier 1930:93–95).

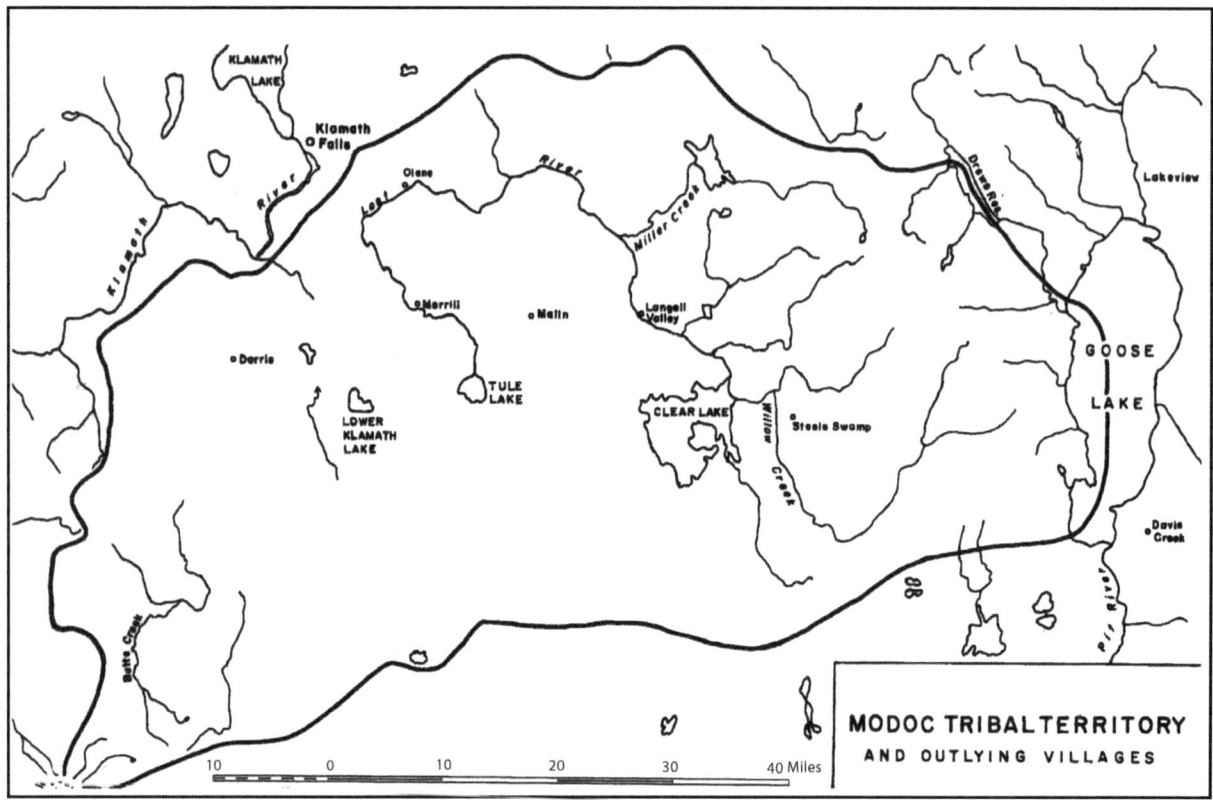

Figure 3: Map of Modoc territory. Note Mt. Shasta in lower left corner. Adapted from Ray (1963:206:Map 1).

The spirits from whom initiates sought power were not specialized. Seekers could gain power for assistance in hunting, gambling, fishing, lovemaking, and warfare with equal expectations from any of the spirit helpers at their disposal (Spier 1930:93). The exception to this was the few specialized spirits available only to shamans. According to Gatschet (1890a:xcviii),

> another class of spirits embodies the spirits of those animals, which have to be consulted by the kiuks or conjurer when he is called to treat a case of disease.³ Such persons only who have been trained during five years for the profession of conjurers can see these spirits, but by them they are seen as clearly as we see the objects around us. To see them they have to go to the home of a deceased conjurer, and at night only. He is then led by a spirit called Yayaya-ash appearing in the form of a one-legged man toward the spot where the animal spirits live; this specter presides over them; there the conjurer notices that each appears different from the other, and is at liberty to consult them about the patient's case. Yayaya-ash means "the frightener," and by the myth tellers is regarded as the Thunder or its spirit.

In order to gain access to this class of spirits, shaman initiates were required to follow a detailed set of procedures. Not only was the nature of this quest different from the ordinary power quest described above, but the way these spirits functioned also differed. Whereas the type of spirit power for ordinary persons was vague and meant only to aid them in succeeding in their various life pursuits, the spirits acquired by shamans served very specific purposes that included curing the sick, controlling the weather, and predicting the future (Gatschet 1890a:104; Ray 1963:81; Spier 1930:103–104). These spirits were considered far too powerful and dangerous for lay persons. Encounters with them, even accidental, might result in illness or death (Ray 1963:41).

Each phase of the shamans' spirit quest was characterized by specific goals: the spiritual call, the acquaintance with the spiritual universe, and finally, the acquisition of particular spirit familiars (Ray 1963:35). The spiritual call came in the form of a dream at any time during a man's life and after menopause in a woman's life. During this dream, "many spirits appeared in kaleidoscopic transition. Upon awakening the dreamer did not remember the identities or characteristics of the spirits, even though the guises in which they appeared were presumably those of animals familiar to him" (Ray 1963:31–32). These dreams continued for about five days, and at their conclusion, the dreamer decided whether or not to pursue training as a shaman (Ray 1963:31–32).

If the seeker decided to pursue training, five more days were devoted to a quest in which personal contact with the spirits was sought. To accomplish this, the seeker visited places where spirits were known to dwell, usually in the early morning and late evening. The most common of these places were the deserted house pits of deceased shamans and the places where they had performed their rituals. "Other spirit sites were the former gathering places of mythological beings, and certain pits and depressions other than those of deserted houses" (Ray 1963:33). At each location seekers would simply lie down and sleep. During their dreams, all the spirits of the universe appeared but did not speak. Most were animals, but some were humans in miniature form. Again the dreamer did not remember the appearance of these spirits, even though these dreams were more vivid than before. By the end of the fifth day, all spirits had passed in review. At this point came the most dramatic event of the quest: "As he stepped into the pit, the seeker fell 'dead,' that is, unconscious" (Ray 1963:33–34).

During this dream, the seeker caught a glimpse of a figure that vaguely resembled a partial human. When it disappeared, the voice of the Ghost Spirit announced to the seeker that he or she would now be a doctor, and then proceeded to give further instructions for the third and final phase of the spirit quest. During this final phase, seekers stayed at home, observed various taboos, and awaited the appearance of specific spirits that visited their dreams. But unlike before, the spirits that appeared were much fewer in number. They appeared individually and spoke directly to the dreamer, each giving specific instructions and a song that the seeker sang immediately upon waking. Family members observing the ritual joined in the singing. As before, this went on for five days. When it was over, the spirits that appeared to the seekers became their "familiars," which the new shamans would use ritually from that point forward (Ray 1963:34–35).

These spirit familiars are the same spirits described above in Gatschet's quote (Gatschet 1890a:xcviii). Through them, shamans performed a variety of services in the community. Their primary role was curing. This was because unexplained illnesses were thought to have a supernatural origin, and people believed that shamans could cure them by using supernatural treatments. When shamans agreed to treat a patient, they dressed in their *mu'lwas,* or "medicine outfits," and went to the patient's home to perform the ritual (Ray 1963:53; Spier 1930:123).[4] During the ritual, they carefully adhered to a strict protocol, beginning with the preparation period, followed by the diagnostic procedure, and concluding with the curing procedure (Ray 1963:55; Spier 1930:122–131). Obtaining a proper diagnosis required the correct assembly of spirit helpers (e.g., familiars). Calling the wrong spirits, or calling spirits out of order, resulted in their failure to affect a cure (Ray 1963:42). Which spirits were called depended on the patient's symptoms.

> A rough correlation was drawn between the characteristics of the animal or objects whose name the spirit bore and the objective symptoms of the disease. Thus Buzzard, since the bird circles over its prey, might be responsible for an illness characterized by dizziness. A correlation was likewise drawn between the characteristics of the spirit and the nature of the curing technique. Thus, if an intrusive object were to be removed, a grasping and tenacious spirit such as Hawk (through analogy with the bird) was used. (Ray 1963:46–47)

Although the Klamath Basin's ethnographic and ethnohistoric literature contains very few references directly related to rock art, the few that exist strongly affiliate it with shamanism (Dennison 1879; Gatschet 1890a:179; Rau 1881:66; Spier 1930:142). In light of the shaman's spirit quest described above, and the extent to which these spirit familiars were necessary for their curing practice, there can be little doubt that much of the rock art on this site depicts these spirits. This has certainly been shown to be the case in much of far western North American rock art, including elsewhere in the Klamath Basin (David 2012a:78; Hann et al. 2010:8; Keyser et al. 2004:74; Whitley 2000:75). The Peninsula's central location in the Modoc world supports this. In myth, it was from this point that the culture hero Kumush created the world and all living things (Ray 1963:18). Later, Kumush was even said to have traveled to The Peninsula to "write" on one of its flat, smooth cliff faces before departing on a journey around the Klamath Basin (Curtin 1884:255). These associations alone indicate that The Peninsula constitutes a spiritually significant point on the landscape where important ritual activities took place, including the creation of rock art. Given its connection with the cosmological underworld described in the Modoc creation narrative (Ray 1963:18), The Peninsula is exactly where shamans would go to seek consultations with the supernatural world. In the following chapters, these factors are considered at length in the interpretation of the 4-Mod-22 petroglyph site.

Chapter 2

Rock Art Recording Methods

Photography

Photography is the most efficient available rock art recording technique (Wainright 1990:56). Not only is it relatively inexpensive, but it also enables researchers to document panels without coming into direct contact with rock surfaces (Swartz 2006:1). We documented petroglyphs at 4-Mod-22 in two phases, during which we used two types of photography.

In Phase I, we established a topographic and horizontal baseline to provide control. Stakes were first placed at every 10 m in a north-south line below the cliff's talus apron. We then placed stakes along the base of the cliff at 10-m intervals precisely at right angles from each of the baseline stakes. Once stakes were in place along the cliff base, the crews mapped the rock face contour against the north-south baseline. The staked intervals along the base of the rock face also helped us to establish 10-m photograph sections that were intended to make management and monitoring efforts relatively easy. Suspected new graffiti or vandalism within a section, for instance, may be compared to the photographs site managers have on file for that particular section.

A stake was placed near a cave-like formation at 100N100W, the southern end of the rock face, where the petroglyphs begin. From there we placed stakes every 10 m north along the base, ending at 190N100W. Once the stakes were in place, digital photographs were taken in Phase II. Following this, we used a GigaPan to capture a detailed image of the entire site from a GPS datum point, which is included in the photograph log. A whiteboard was used for the beginning and ending shots in order to keep track of the photographs within each 10-m section.

Once back in the lab, we converted the photos from RAW to JPEG format and uploaded them to the GigaPan website—information in one digital folder and the JPEGs in another. All of the close-up shots were gathered into digital folders with labels corresponding to the section of the capture. Each entry on the photograph log explained the method of naming and filing used for the photos. The photographer, MaKai Magié, retained a copy of the JPEGs and RAW photos as a backup measure.

Follow-up Photographs

The project goal was to create a photographic record of the site that can be used to easily spot and investigate graffiti and vandalism. One of the fallouts from using this technique was that few photographs were taken of complete petroglyph compositions. Instead, fragments of these compositions ended up in different locations of the photograph record because they occurred in more than one staked section. To correct this, we made a follow-up site visit on December 28, 2013, to photograph selected complete compositions and images where this had occurred. A Nikon D40 digital camera was used at varying ranges. No GPS was taken of the photograph points. We added the photos to the inventory created by Makai Magié, and a record of them was included the photograph log as an addendum.

GigaPan Capture of 4-Mod-22

GigaPan is a robot that attaches to a regular digital camera, allowing site recorders to take multiple overlapping close-up pictures of a site. Afterward the individual pictures are stitched together into one large formatted picture that is then uploaded to the GigaPan website. The GigaPan capture was done with a 200–400-mm lens. The use of a GigaPan to capture 4-Mod-22 was for both research and archival purposes. On the website viewers can zoom in or out of the photo and still retain clarity. This is an especially important feature in terms of site monitoring and management. With the GigaPan Capture of 4-Mod-22, monitors can see the whole rock face and surrounding apron and then zoom in on it with such clarity that they can make out the details of the rock art and graffiti. By capturing the entire site and uploading it, one is able to access the site remotely. Site managers and researchers can also use GigaPan to compare data in the field to see if any new graffiti or vandalism has occurred simply by bringing along a device capable of internet access. The GigaPan can also be shared, thus allowing others to access the content of the site without causing further damage to the site itself.

In addition to the rock face, we also took GigaPan shots in front of sections 100N100W, 110N100W, and 120N100W in hope of capturing clearer images. We also collected GPS data for each photo point position, and these data are included in the photograph log. This could have been more successful with the use of the 100–400-mm lens, which would have captured better exposure. Finally, we took a 360-degrees panorama of the area from the original location in order to show the surrounding terrain.

Close-ups Capture of MOD-22

Digital pictures of the rock features were taken using the Canon EOS 30D from the baseline working from top to bottom, left to right. Efforts were made to overlap as much as possible and to capture isolates to be documented later by others. Most of these were taken with the 28–135-mm zoom, except for the cave/concave feature at 100N100W and the cave/concave feature at 150N100W.

After reviewing the GigaPan website and close-up shots, we came to the conclusion that using both methods was ideal for documenting the site. The GigaPan allows for close-up viewing without being at the site. The drawback is that the GigaPan website can be slow or nonresponsive. It is best to view the site using a large screen computer capable of fast processing speeds and a good Internet connection.

Tracings

Following the field portion of the project, we completed tracings in the lab only for analytical purposes and because they are easier to tabulate than photographs. These were traced directly from digital images. No scales were used in either the photography or the tracings. Future work on this site should include both scaled photographs and tracings. Beside helping to establish the relative sizes of the imagery, it will greatly assist in establishing a motif count that can be compared to the Petroglyph Point materials that Heizer and Clewlow (1973) and Crotty (1981) gathered.

Interpretive Methods

Ethnography

There are numerous potential hazards researchers must face when incorporating ethnography into rock art research. One that is most frequently cited is the incompleteness of the ethnographic record (David and Keyser 2008:26). In the Klamath Basin, ethnographic references to rock art are conspicuously scarce at best, and direct references to Modoc rock art are nonexistent. The ethnographic information on rock art that is available in the greater Klamath Basin is often fragmentary, incomplete, and shrouded in cultural metaphors. A very effective way to fill in the missing information in local ethnography is to make ethnographic analogies with neighboring groups who bore significant cultural and linguistic similarities (Loubser and Whitley 1999:1:48).

Although the Klamath and Modoc diverged into two distinct political entities around A.D. 1780 (Gatschet 1890a:13), they maintained similarities in almost all significant aspects, including their spiritual beliefs and practices (Loubser and Whitley 1999:1:48). Ethnographic information from both of these groups forms a mutually complementary information set that can provide a wider framework through which more specific references in any single ethnography might be interpreted. Based in part on this information set, a number of researchers have shown that Klamath-Modoc rock art has strong ties to shamanism, supernatural potency, and power questing (Crotty 1981; David 2005, 2010, 2012a, 2012b; David and Keyser 2008; David and Morgan 2014; Hann and Bettles 2006; Lee et al. 1988; Whitley et al. 2004). Thus it is within this context that we must seek out a more complete understanding of the art and its origins.

An especially useful body of research in psychology led to the publication of an interpretive framework that has significantly advanced rock art interpretation and method. In the North American far west, this neuropsychological model has been especially useful in two main areas. First, it has provided significant insights into certain types of rock art associated with trance. Second, it has helped to clarify vague and fragmentary statements made about trance experiences and rock art in extant ethnographic texts (Whitley 1994).

The Neuropsychological Model

Lewis-Williams and Dowson (1988) based their neuropsychological model on experiments conducted in psychology that began in the late nineteenth century and cross-cultural descriptions of trance. The focus of these experiments was to understand the way that the human brain reacted to induced altered states of consciousness (ASC), or trance. From these experiments emerged important patterns in the visual and somatic precepts that human subjects reported experiencing during these altered states. Klüver (1926, 1942:177, cited in Lewis-Williams and Dowson 1988:202) abstracted redundant elements from laboratory subjects and concluded that the visual precepts they witnessed during ASC had constant forms. Some years later, Horowitz (1975:178, cited in Lewis-Williams and Dowson 1988:202) independently arrived at the same conclusions. Other researchers confirmed their findings and identified yet more redundant forms that included grids, zigzags, dots, spirals, and nested curves ([see Figure 4] Eichmeier and Höfer 1974; Horowitz 1964; Knoll 1958; Richards 1971; Siegel 1977, cited in Lewis-Williams and Dowson 1988:202).

These entoptic phenomena are basic geometric shapes generated within the optic nerve during the initial stages of ASC (Tyler 1978:1633). Two classes of entoptic phenomena occur. Phosphenes, which can be generated by applying pressure to the eye, form constants that derive from the optic system itself. Both phosphenes and entoptic phenomena form the building blocks for the hallucinations that occur in the later stages of ASC. Because the nervous systems of all *Homo sapiens* are hard wired the same, and this has remained unchanged for the past 100,000 years or more, people all over the world experience altered states of consciousness in a similar way and have done so throughout their history as a species (Lewis-Williams and Dowson 1988:202).

The model's application to rock art studies is premised on the notion that, by definition, shamanism required trance (Whitley 1994:8). In shamanic societies, entering an altered state of consciousness was believed to be an encounter with the supernatural world. The entoptic images people witnessed were thought to be visions of this world. The neuropsychological model, in this regard, provides a "middle range" that effectively bridges the mental imagery witnessed during trance with rock art where these geometrical forms are depicted.

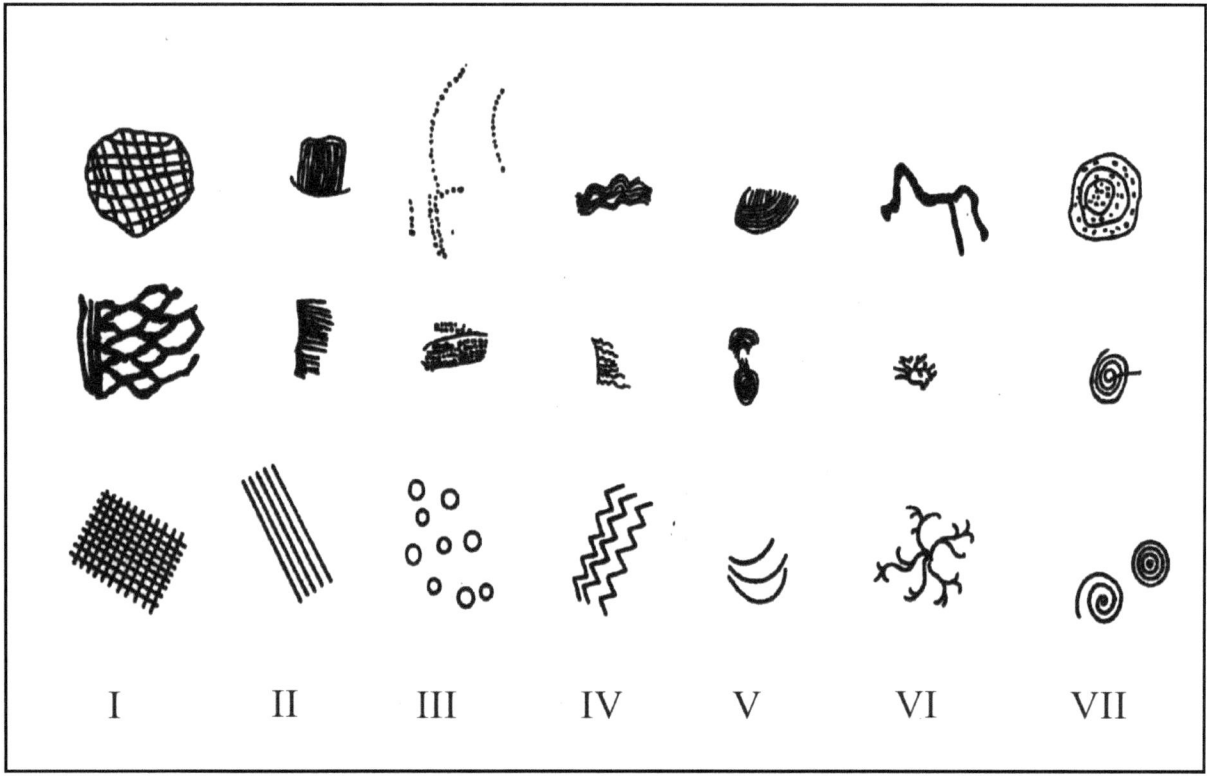

Figure 4: The seven recurring entoptic forms, the first component of Lewis-Williams and Dowson's (1988) neuropsychological model. The top row provides idealized entoptic patterns. The middle and bottom rows are examples using Numic petroglyphs from the Coso Range, California. The seven entoptic forms are: I) grids; II) parallel lines; III) dots and flecks; IV) zigzags; V) nested curves; VI) filigrees and meanders; and VII) cortices. Reproduced from Whitley (1994:Figure 1) with permission of author.

The geometric forms that bombard the subject's mental vision during ASC are governed by seven principles of perception: replication, fragmentation, integration, superpositioning, juxtapositioning, reduplication, and rotation. Under replication, the subject perceives entoptic visions in their basic, fundamental forms. Fragmentation occurs when these forms are broken down into minimal components. Instead of witnessing a grid, for example, a subject may only witness a ladder form or a single square. Integration occurs when these images (fragmented or complete) combine with other entoptics to form more complex patterns, such as a series of parallel lines whose ends transform into zigzags. Superpositioning and juxtapositioning occur when one image appears on top of another or beside it, respectively. Reduplication occurs when an image becomes a series of similar or identical images. A single line, for instance, might become a series of parallel lines, or a single circle may become a series of circles spanning the subject's field of vision. Finally, entoptic images may rotate in the subject's field of vision (Lewis-Williams and Dowson 1988:203).

During the trance experience, the mental imagery occurs in three broadly defined stages. In Stage 1, subjects experience entoptic phenomena alone. Because they all derive from the central nervous system, these images cannot be controlled by the subject (Lewis-Williams and Dowson 1988:203; Siegel and Jarvik 1975). The seven most commonly occurring entoptic forms in Figure 4 are hardwired in the nervous system of all *Homo sapiens*. In Stage 2, subjects try to make sense of these entoptic images by transforming them into iconic forms, or images that they recognize. "In a normal state of consciousness, the brain decodes the constant stream of sense impressions it receives by matching it against its store of knowledge" (Lewis-Williams and Dowson 1988:203). During ASC, however, the nervous system governs this function (Heinze 1986:154). As a result, zigzag lines may come to represent snakes, lightning, a skyline, or ocean waves, depending largely on the subject's mood at the time and set of internal priorities. During Stage 3, subjects reported being surrounded by a vortex with a grid-like pattern marking its sides. Simultaneously, they experienced "a progressive exclusion of perceptual information" as they are drawn deeper into the trance experience (Horowitz 1975:178). According to Siegel and Jarvik, it is upon those "screens" that iconic hallucinations first appear (Siegel 1977:136 cited in Lewis-Williams and Dowson 1988; Siegel and Jarvik 1975:127, 143). As the shift to iconic imagery deepens, the subject's perceptions become more vivid. "Subjects under laboratory conditions [in Stage 3] stopped using similes to describe their experiences and asserted that the images are indeed what they appear to be" (Siegel and Jarvik 1975:128). The distinction between iconic hallucinations and reality observed in previous states disappeared. At peak hallucinatory periods, "subjects begin to feel dissociated from their bodies and frequently become part of their own imagery" (Lewis-Williams and Dowson 1988:211). They refer to this condition as *participation*.

Notably, although it does appear that exclusively entoptic imagery occurs in the first stage, these three stages are cumulative rather than sequential. Entoptic phenomena may persist during all stages of the trance experience. Iconic forms seen in the later stages of trance are often "projected against a background of geometric [entoptic] forms" (Siegel 1977:134 cited in Lewis-Williams and Dowson 1988). In this frame of mind, the range of perceptions subjects may experience is limited only by the cultural experience acting on them and by the range of visual perceptions generated by the nervous system (Lewis-Williams and Dowson 1988:204). Figure 5 shows how a Westerner might experience the three stages of a trance.

The neuropsychological model is especially useful in helping researchers to identify the origins of certain categories of rock art that otherwise might defy explanation. While this is not meant to suggest that all geometric figures on a site be classified as entoptic phenomena, the model can certainly be used to bolster ethnographic accounts of rock art in communities where shamanic trance was known to exist. By extension, based on the premise that the brains of all *Homo sapiens* are hardwired to experience trance in similar ways, the model can bring an informed approach into the study of rock art where no ethnography is available. In the Klamath Basin, where ethnographic references to rock art are minimal and vague, but where references to shamanism and trance are especially rich, it is possible to make informed interpretations of the art based on the expectations of this model.

Use of Myth

As an extension of ethnography, myth is fast becoming an indispensable information source for understanding Klamath-Modoc spirituality and rock art. Every aspect of the shamans' enterprise is described and codified in Klamath-Modoc myth. Not only does it identify the various important characters that functioned as shamans' spirit helpers, it also describes in detail their primary roles. Specific spirits like Kumush, Skoks, and Yahyahyaas are identified as particularly potent spirits reputed to be capable of reversing otherwise certain death. Supernatural events leading to miraculous creations, such as The Peninsula and Crater Lake, or the quelling of mischievous spirits like Wulkutska, served to structure the ritual acts of shamans who emulated these powerful beings in efforts to perform miracles of their own. The world of myth, then, was the world of shamans.

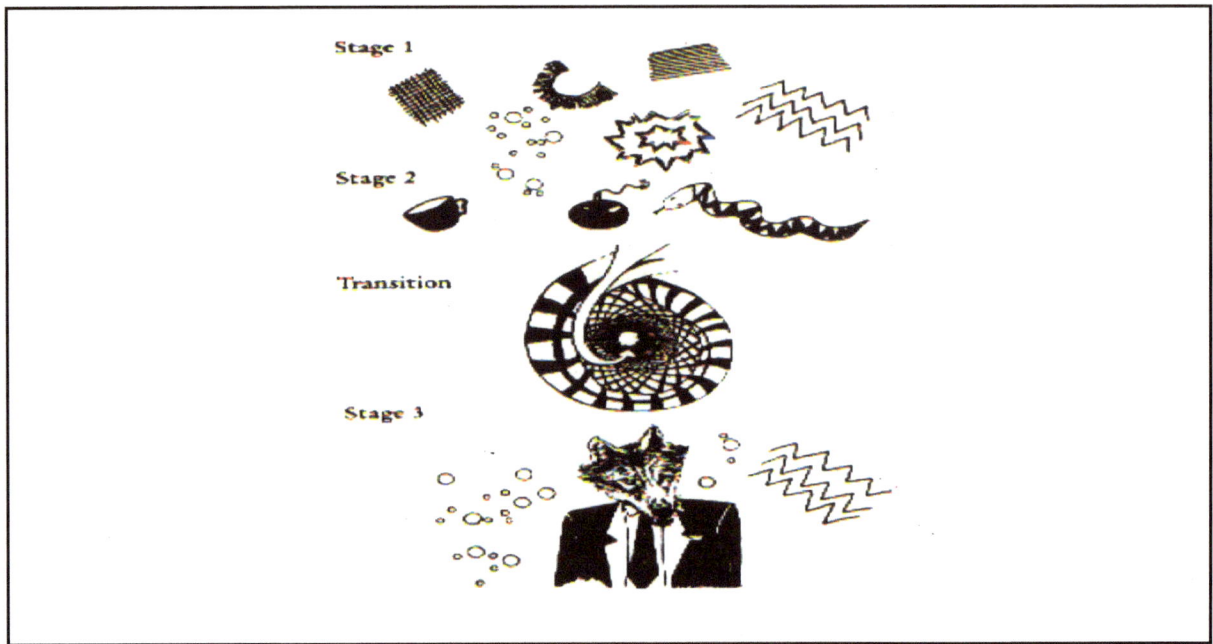

Figure 5: The three stages of the neuropsychological model as a Westerner might perceive it. Reproduced from Lewis-Williams (2001:Figure 12.2) with author's permission.

Much of the shaman's power derived from the fact that these stories were both understood and, to some extent, believed by ordinary villagers. With the periodic telling and retelling of these stories, knowledge and understanding were maintained. At the same time, shamans wasted no opportunity to display their supernatural potency to the villagers, either through ritual acts, ostentatious lodge décor, elaborate public ceremonies like the winter performance, or by claiming credit for otherwise natural phenomena (Ray 19 63:37–41; Spier 1930:105, 109–118). The peoples' belief in the shamans' supernatural abilities thus went hand-in-hand with their familiarity with the myths. For this reason, myth is regarded here as a critical enabling mechanism for shamanistic practice. It is considered neither a true nor untrue representation of the past. Regarding myth in this fashion ignores the fact that it played an essential role in perpetuating ideology, not only by encoding important customs and beliefs but also by motivating behaviors that left archaeological traces, such as ritual objects and rock art. Rather than attempt to evaluate its legitimacy as source of scientific data as Mason (2000) and Echo-hawk (2000) have discussed, it is deemed more useful to discover the extent to which Klamath-Modoc ancestors believed these tales and as a result engaged in rituals that produced datable material culture. Its applicability to rock art is especially important and will be evaluated in detail in the following chapters.

Temporality

Another major pitfall that researchers encounter when using ethnography or mythology to interpret the archaeological past is *temporality*. In the Klamath Basin, rock art has been shown to date between 4500 B.P. (Lee and Hyder 1990:200) and historic times (Rau 1881:65). The myths used in this analysis were collected by Curtin (1884) and Gatschet (1890a) at the same time the historic period rock art was produced. This raises the possibility that strong interpretive models derived from myth can be created for the historic period rock art and then projected back into the prehistoric past. How far back in time this can extend is difficult to say because such limitations have not been defined. According to Whitley (1982:266),

> while some controversy exists concerning the length of time during which an oral tradition is thought to persist, with some folklorists arguing for a relatively short time span (cf. Raglan 1960), Pendergast and Meighan (1959) have substantiated the notion that such traditions can last for an extended period. They cite a specific example to support the contention that certain Paiute traditions of southern Utah may be almost a millennium in age.

In the Klamath Basin, oral narratives might extend much farther back than a millennium, even though outside ideologies may have influenced them throughout the historic period. Such instances, however, do not necessarily affect cultural systems in negative ways. As Horton (1982) has pointed out, the cognitive and symbolic systems of traditional, small-scale societies are commonly "open" in such a way as to accommodate rather than reject new ideas, beliefs, gods, and rituals. Cultural elements that Westerners might assume to have been compromised with the introduction of new ideas would not so much have been lost as they would have been incorporated. New cultural elements would have simply been accepted into pre-existing structures without replacing them (Whitley et al. 2004:234). In this way, symbolic systems do not lose their internal structure by accommodating variation. Instead, variation serves to reinforce that structure with new expressions.

Another important factor to consider is that myth existed within a web of relationships. While no mechanism outside of human memory ensured that myths would be recalled using a previous teller's exact words, the web of relationships supporting them ensured that their fundamental components would survive. An important key to their longevity in the Klamath Basin was the landscape itself. Klamath Basin myths teem not only with important myth-inspired place-names for special localities but also the stories that made those places spiritually significant. In one story concerning the origins of Crater Lake, for example, a battle between the chiefs of the Lower and Upper worlds threatened to wipe out the people who lived in the valleys below. The Chief of the Lower World rose out of a deep crack in Mt. Mazama, while the Chief of the Upper World towered over Mt. Shasta. As they engaged in battle, the ground shook, and red-hot boulders hurtled through the skies. Realizing that only a human sacrifice would quell the anger of these spirit chiefs, two of the eldest medicine men climbed the slopes of the mountain that was to become Crater Lake and threw themselves down into the fiery pit. With their sacrifice, the destruction ceased. The Chief of the Lower World was driven to his home under the mountain, and the mountain then fell in upon him. By morning, the mountain was gone. And in the ensuing years rain filled the crater with water, and it became Crater Lake (Clark 1953:53–55).

Several important mnemonic factors derive from this story. Not only does it appear to preserve the eruption of Mt. Mazama from 7000 B.P. but it also points to the spiritual causation behind it according to the beliefs of the Klamath and Modoc. At some point in time, the people came to see Crater Lake as a place that harbored great supernatural power, and shamans or shaman initiates would venture there to swim in its waters and stack rocks at night in the hope of tapping into that power (Ray 1963:81; Spier 1930:98). In short, this oral tradition, preserved as myth, identified a significant spiritual place on the landscape (Crater Lake) and as a result influenced a ritual behavior (e.g., vision questing), which resulted in tangible material culture (rock cairns). The relationship between the oral traditions and the web of encoding mechanisms worked tangentially to preserve the integrity of the story.

Aided by a consistent landscape, there is little reason to believe that the sacred geography, as identified in myth, did not aid in the preservation of a mythic tradition that extended well into the remote past. The Klamath and Modoc have occupied this region for at least the past 10,000 years (Cressman 1956:470). As Whitley et al. (2004:230–231) have demonstrated, rock art sites correspond well with the sacred landscape as defined by myth. The presence of rock art dating back millennia at some of these locations suggests that these places have been sacred, and codified as such in myth, for at least as long as the rock art has been present but probably much longer. Thus, passed on through oral traditions, myths were not free-floating phenomena, losing integrity through each transmission. They were stored on the named landscape, preserved in ritual, and embedded in the collective consciousness of the group. Despite variations in the telling and retelling of these sacred stories, this network of natural and cultural storage devices preserved their fundamental structure and functioned as a prosthetic that enhanced and expanded human memory.

CHAPTER 3

Analysis
Motifs, Markings, and Figures

Klamath Basin rock art is overtly abstract in nature and largely comprised of geometric motifs that emphasize circular figures, parallel lines, and zigzag and wavy lines. Representational elements are almost entirely absent. Human figures, though rare, do occur, but depictions of game animals are completely absent (Crotty 1981:159–161). Earlier writers argued for a Great Basin influence in the art (Heizer and Clewlow 1973; Grant 1967; Steward 1929), but this has been rejected in more recent studies based mainly on the absence of representations of big game animals upon which much of the Great Basin Style was premised (Lee et al. 1988:133). Because of the unique preponderance and distribution of certain critical elements, such as concentric circles and zigzag motifs, more recent researchers have argued instead for a unique Klamath Basin Style (Crotty 1981:160; Swartz 1998:120; Hann et al. 2010:2).

The rock art of 4-Mod-22 is comprised entirely of petroglyphs arranged on the single rock face that runs the entire length of the site. The sandstone-like texture of the rock face suggests the possibility that prehistoric artists created some of the figures by scratching the rock with their bare fingers (Hann and Bettles 2006:186), while others were likely made with the assistance of a narrow stone, stick, or bone fragment. Some images were incised with a narrow edge, and holes were drilled into the rock presumably with an instrument resembling the prehistoric fire drill. Drilled-hole diameters range in size from not much wider than a Q-Tip to more than two centimeters.

The most common images on the site are concentrations of zigzags, drilled holes, and rows of parallel lines 2–30 cm in length. A few of the panels are completely filled with these markings, with other motif types intermixed throughout. The petroglyphs can be grouped into three basic categories: iconic motifs, residual markings, and geometric figures. Iconic motifs are images that represent culturally identifiable objects or beings. Residual markings are comprised of the large concentrations of zigzags, parallel lines, and drilled holes that, as a single category, largely define the petroglyph assemblage on this site. These are distinguished from the other categories not only by their pervasiveness but also by their intent. They are the result of repeated behaviors that left residual traces. But in spite of their similarity to some of the iconic and geometric varieties, the act of creating them was considered more important than executing a final design. This distinction will be made more apparent in the following chapter. Finally, geometric figures are symbols that do not represent items or beings found in the natural world. To this extent, many may be regarded as entoptic in origin.

Two of the site's three caves contain petroglyphs. The images in the first are of the same general style found elsewhere on the site. The similarity suggests that the artists regarded this cave with no more importance than the rest of the site. The images in the second, however, are comprised almost completely of circles. This difference suggests that it may have held special significance. Unlike circular motifs elsewhere on the site, these circles are all single and unelaborated. Signs of water erosion on their edges suggest the cave was inundated for a period of time subsequent to their creation.

The overtly abstract nature of the 4-Mod-22 petroglyphs is consistent with that of the Klamath Basin as a whole, although it appears to represent a more archaic expression of that style. This often makes it difficult to differentiate iconic from geometric figures. What compounds this confusion further is the widespread use of synecdoche, in which subjects, reduced to their most minimal components, are meant to represent the whole. To some extent, identification of certain motifs was possible only through very close scrutiny coupled with information provided by ethnography and myth.

Images that appear below are intended to represent the range of artistic variation displayed on this site. Because of their number and density on the site, individual images were not measured, and a motif count was not attempted for the present study. Finally, throughout this analysis I frequently note where the motifs depicted on 4-Mod-22 appear at other Klamath Basin rock art sites.

Iconic Motifs

The iconic motifs identified on this site include circles, sunbursts, skeletal figures, anthropomorphic figures, spirit beings, rattlesnakes, and triangles. These motifs vary in size and placement; some are large and conspicuous, and others are small and difficult to distinguish from the engravings within which they are integrated. Many of the iconic motifs in the 4-Mod-22 assemblage are well-established motifs at rock art sites throughout the Klamath Basin.

Circles and Sunbursts

Circles and Sunbursts are among the most widely depicted images in Klamath Basin rock art, and they comprise the majority of the iconic motifs on 4-Mod-22 (Figure 6). Although circular figures have elsewhere been categorized as "geometric," this symbol is associated with an actual mythological being in the Klamath Basin, and thus it has been classified as iconic.

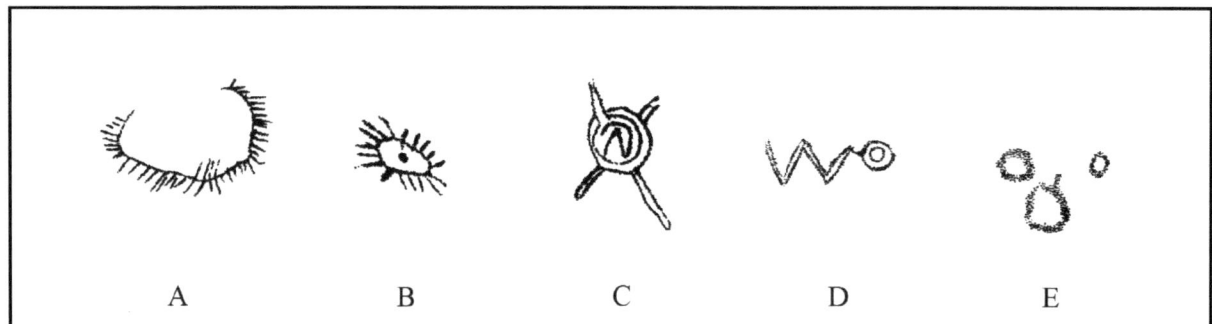

Figure 6: Sample of cicrular figures from 4-Mod-22. Tracings by Robert David.

Circular figures range from small, simple circles that appear either alone or in small groups (Figure 6E) to rayed sunbursts that exhibit elaborate, internal ornamentation (Figure 6C). The range of variation shown in Figure 6 is, by and large, duplicated at Petroglyph Point (Crotty 1981:157) and frequently shows up at both open-air sites and within the lava tubes in Lava Beds National Monument. The nucleated, concentric-circle variety, as later shown in Figure 29 in Chapter 4, are more commonly depicted at open-air sites, and are typically larger than those found within the lava tubes or more culturally isolated locales (see Loring and Loring 1983:26–30). Ethnohistoric evidence suggests that the most frequent use of this motif occurred in the late prehistoric and protohistoric periods (Dennison 1879; Rau 1881:65).

The curious motif shown in Figure 6C, in spite of its odd appearance, is comprised of elements that are commonly associated with circular figures elsewhere in Klamath Basin rock art. The internal designs are made up of a second circle and the beginning of a third circle that morphs into a zigzag. Basically, this is the same "tailed" circle that appears in 6D, with its elements reconfigured.

Skeletal Figures

The skeletal figures on this site appear with only slightly less frequency than the circles and sunbursts. Most are made up of a single vertical line that bisects a series of chevrons arranged to symbolize ribs (Figure 7). These figures are small and often integrated with the site's more pervasive "residual" elements, making them difficult to spot. Nonetheless, their high frequency suggests that they served an important ritual role.

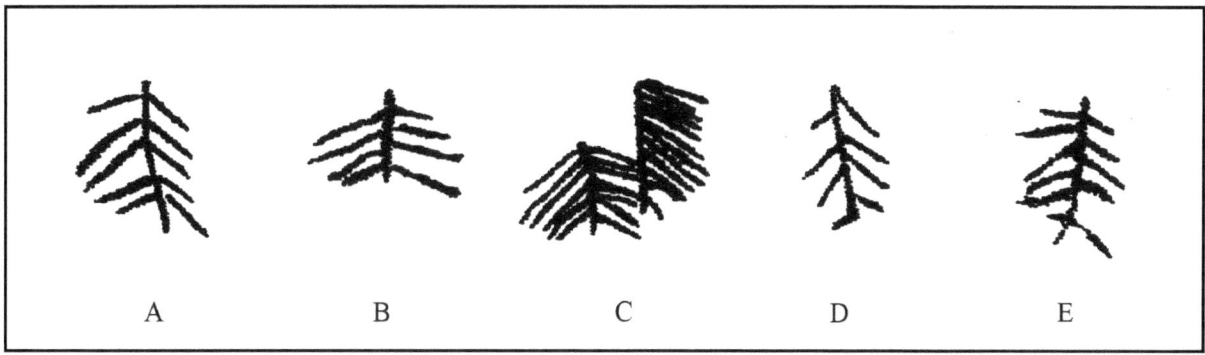

Figure 7: Sample of skeletal figures from 4-Mod-22. Tracings by Robert David.

Skeletal figures are common throughout the Klamath Basin, and they occur in both isolated and outdoor contexts that are closely associated with villages and major camps. Those that are located in more public domains tend to exhibit more recognizable anthropomorphic characteristics (see David 2012a:69). Similar figures at Petroglyph Point appear at a frequency that is on par with 4-Mod-22, many of which are depicted with more recognizable anthropomorphic and "insect-like' characteristics (Crotty 1981:157–158).

Anthropomorphic Figures

Anthropomorphic figures comprise another large image category on 4-Mod-22 (Figure 8). Like the skeletal figures, many are comparatively small and situated less conspicuously on the rock face than other motifs, making their frequency not apparent at first. None are depicted in completely human form. Some appear as simple stick figures, while others are somewhat therianthropic (Figure 8E). Figures 8I–8K are similar to images elsewhere that were known to serve as metaphors for the magical flight of shamans in trance (Lewis-Williams 2001:342; Whitley 1994:16–19). The largest of these, Figures 8B–8D, are among the few that can be considered full-bodied anthropomorphs, as they exhibit digits on both hands and feet. They are part of a larger composition that includes a decorated zigzag symbol deeply engraved into the rock's surface just above. A photograph of this composition is later shown in Figure 43 in Chapter 4.

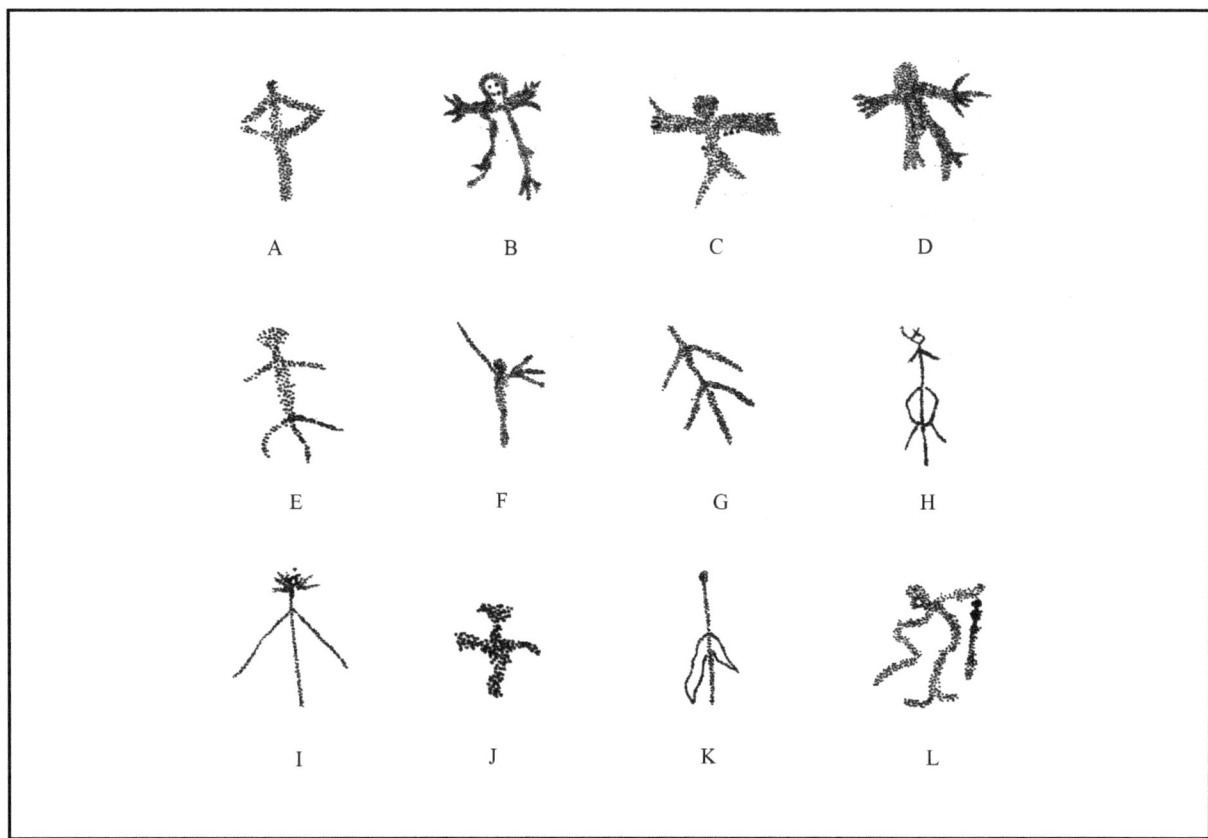

Figure 8: Sample of anthropomorphic figures from 4-Mod-22. Tracings by Robert David.

Figures 8E, 8G, 8H, and 8K exhibit either phallic elements or tails. Although phallic elements are more common in the Klamath Basin where human figures have been stylized (see for example, Crotty 1981:151, Figure 5b), the "tailed" variety is more common in the eastern portions of the Klamath-Modoc territory where Great Basin influences may have affected local styles. Elsewhere in the Klamath Basin, anthropomorphic figures occur in both isolated and open-air contexts. Those in the more secluded sites tend to be small and widely stylized, while those at the open-air sites ranged from stick-bodied (David 2012b:55–56) to full-bodied figures (Loring and Loring 1983:19, Figure A) with minimal elaboration.

Spirit Figures

Spirit figures are slightly anthropomorphic, but were stylized so dramatically that they could not be considered human depictions. They are essentially comprised of two crosshatched lines with some possible anthropomorphic features added. Only three of these motifs were noted on this site (Figure 9). A somewhat similar motif appearing at Petroglyph Point may depict a variation of these figures (Figure 10). The simplest, Figure 9B exhibits the suggestion of a head while Figure 9A shows what may be taken as eyes and extremities tipped with digits. Figure 9C is the most basic of the three, comprised of the typical crosshatched lines with a chevron "cap." The terminal ends are rounded at the top and may have been intended to represent eyes.

No figures like this have been noted in the caves recorded by Loubser and Whitley (1999), or in Mod-17, recorded by Lee et al. (1988). It is entirely possible that this motif represents an archaic expression that either evolved into other forms or disappeared altogether in later times. It is equally possible that this motif represents a new expression that emerged near the advent of the Klamath Indian Reservation and a new way of life.

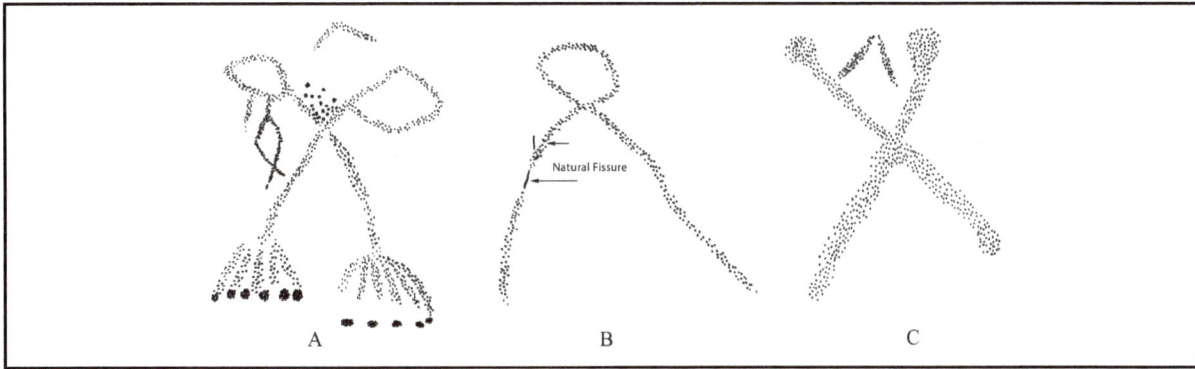

Figure 9: Spirit figures from 4-Mod-22. Tracings by Robert David.

Figure 10: Spirit figure from Petroglyph Point. Photo by Robert David.

Rattlesnakes

Rattlesnakes appear in various places on the site and often take on the form of zigzags, diamond patterns, and enclosed segmented lines meant to simulate rattles (Figure 11). It is entirely possible that more rattlesnakes are depicted on this site. Zigzags and diamond patterns appear in just about every imaginable form. However, zigzags could just as easily symbolize lightning or even water as it might a rattlesnake, and in some contexts they may even simply express supernatural power.

Zigzags appearing by themselves or not associated with any other rattlesnake attributes were not identified in this report as rattlesnake figures.

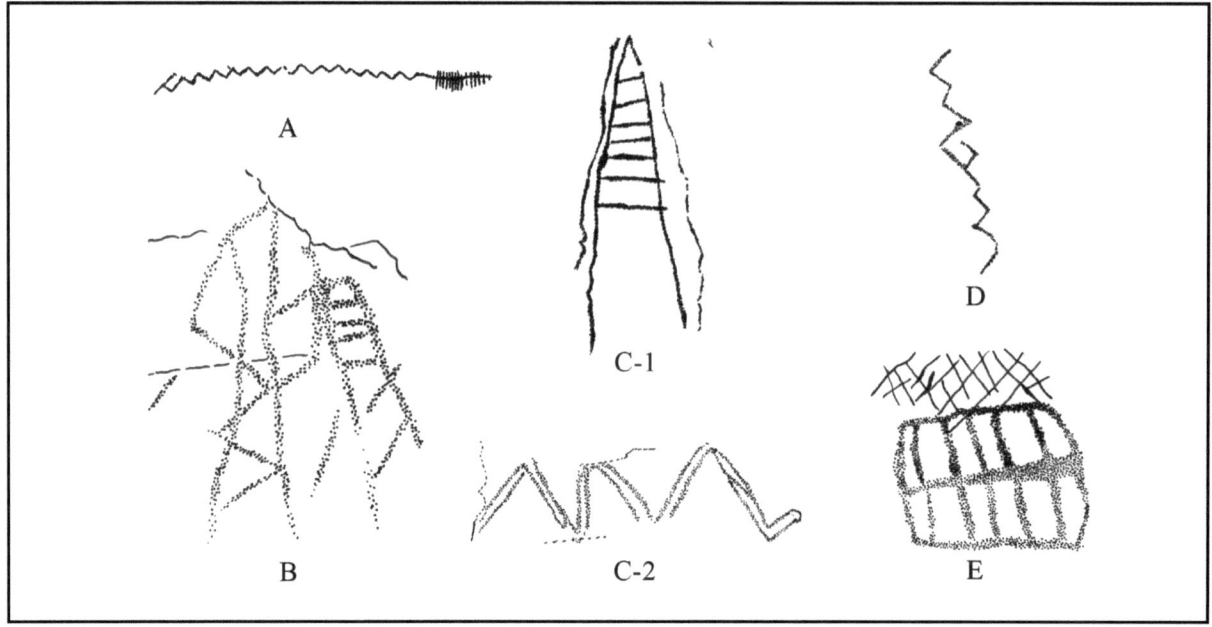

Figure 11: Sample of rattlesnake figures from 4-Mod-22. Tracings by Robert David.

Figure 11A shows a rare, complete depiction of a rattlesnake rendered in stick-bodied form. Figure 11B shows the stylized head of a rattlesnake juxtaposed with its rattle directly on the right. The rest of the body is missing at exactly the point where the rock face changes texture and coloration. A series of zigzags were used to emulate the snake's markings. Note also that the artist utilized the diagonal fissure in the rock face either to form a portion of rattlesnake's head or, for reasons discussed in the next chapter, to show the rattlesnake entering the rock, as the creature's habit dictates. In Figure 11C, different parts of a single rattlesnake appear in two places on the rock's surface. Figure 11C-1 depicts an exaggerated rattle, while 11C-2 shows the snake's zigzag body with a head that has been drastically de-emphasized. The tail has been outlined by another engraved line. This may have been an attempt to depict it in the act of rattling, or simply to enhance its importance. Either explanation would be consistent with the interpretations presented in the next chapter. Figure 11D depicts a zigzag snake design with a diamond-shaped head and elongated protruding tongue that, like Figure 11A, is depicted in stick-bodied fashion. Notably, the use of an incomplete diamond to symbolize the head is a common artistic convention in this region, where stick-bodied snakes occur with heads shown. No rattles in this depiction are present, suggesting that it may represent a different species of snake, or that the artist simply chose not to depict them. Figure 11E, like 11C-1, shows an exaggerated rattle associated with a curious diamond pattern that probably symbolizes a rattlesnake's skin.

Any of the numerous zigzag or wavy lines that appear at Petroglyph Point may have been intended to depict snakes of any kind. However, none of these depictions bear the same or similar rattlesnake attributes that occur at 4-Mod-22. The same is true for the paintings located in the nearby lava tubes and at open-air sites. The only complete (and recognizable) rattlesnake depiction in the vicinity of 4-Mod-22 is the coiled specimen painted at SIS-288 in Figure 12. This figure is stylistically similar to Figure 11B.

Figure 12: Coiled rattlesnake motif from SIS-288. Notably, the convex rock face gives the impression of a rattlesnake sitting with its head resting on top of its coiled body. Photo by Robert David.

Triangles

The numerous triangles depicted on this site appear alone, in groups, or in association with circular motifs (Figure 13) and are common motifs in Klamath Basin rock art (Swartz 1998:120). Like the circles and sunbursts, these figures are associated directly with a mythological character and are thus reported here as iconic rather than geometric forms. As the examples show, they can appear alone or in small groups, with or without internal ornamentations, or even superimposed with patterns of drilled holes, as shown in Figure 13D.

Triangles appear all over the Klamath Basin and are very common at public sites (David 2012a:55–85). Sometimes they are depicted as the "head" of stick-bodied animals (Figure 14) or other times as stylized anthropomorphic figures (Figure 15). They are frequently associated with circular motifs. Smaller depictions of this motif appear at Petroglyph Point in similar proportions.

Residual Markings

The images identified on 4-Mod-22 as residual markings include repeated zigzags, rows of parallel lines, and fields of drilled holes. What distinguishes them from the other categories is that they appear in large concentrations on this site and by far are the most pervasive. These are deeply integrated with iconic motifs but sometimes appear in isolated concentrations of their own. They are also frequently superimposed over iconic figures and in a few cases were used to create iconic motifs themselves.

The behaviors that produced these markings are distinguished in two important ways. First, it is apparent that much more focus and intensity was required to create them than the iconic or geometric varieties. Second, with the possible exception of the large zigzag concentrations and a few of the patterns created by drilled holes, the artists did not seem overly concerned with using them to create motifs. What appears most important was the act of creating them.

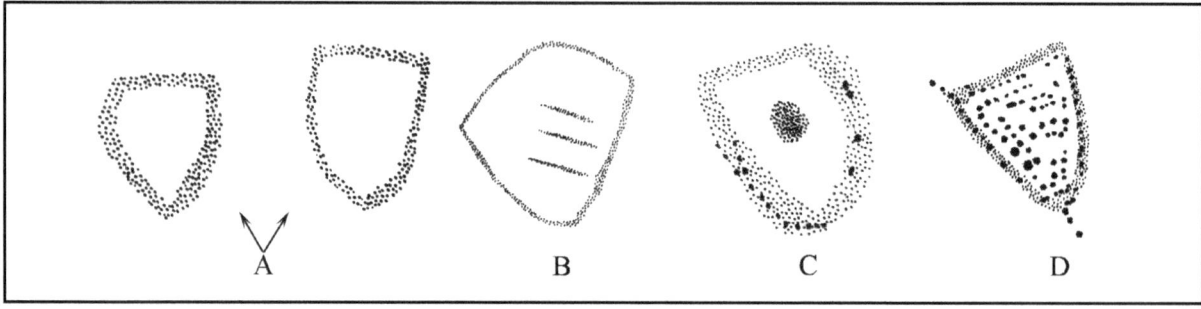

Figure 13: Sample of triangular figures from 4-Mod-22. Tracings by Robert David.

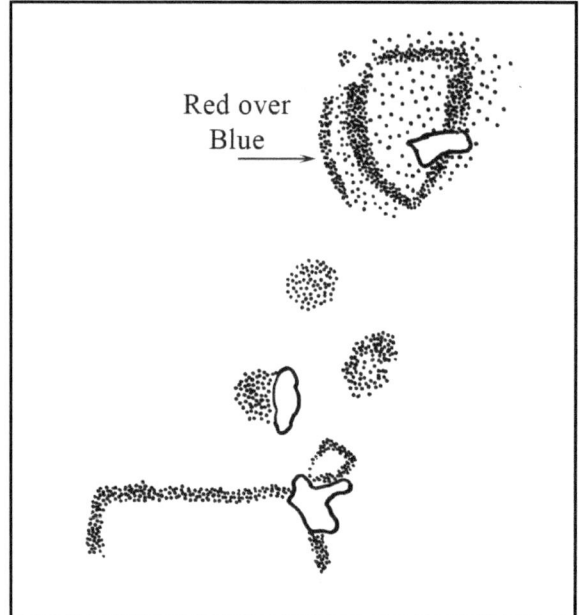

Figure 14: The triangular figure on the top depicts the head of Tskel, the mythical pine marten. The line on the left is probably Tskel's medicine stick. The image on the bottom depicts the marten's head and body in stick-figure form. Tracings by Robert David.

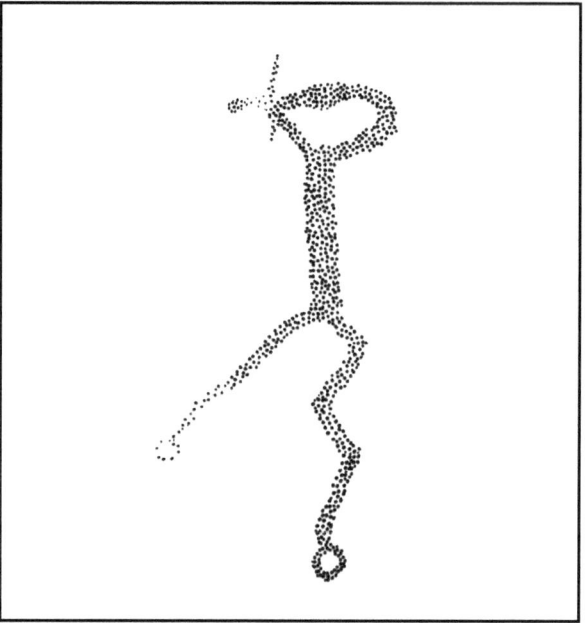

Figure 15: Anthropomorphized depiction of Tskel, the mythical pine marten spirit. Note the medicine stick on the side of his head. Tracing by Melissa Morgan.

Zigzag Concentrations

Large zigzag concentrations appear all over 4-Mod-22 and often cover entire rock panels, as shown in Figure 16. They differ from the rattlesnakes and the paired zigzags (described below) in that they typically larger, appear in higher concentrations, and are heavily integrated with drilled holes and rows of engraved lines. In general, zigzags appear at most Klamath Basin rock art sites. The painted variety is especially concentrated in caves and sites in relatively isolated contexts. Yet even the sites where they appear with the most frequency would be hard pressed to match the density in which they are represented at 4-Mod-22 and Petroglyph Point. This suggests that The Peninsula itself played some role in the artists' impulse to depict them at these locations.

Figure 16: This large rock section from 4-Mod-22 is covered with carved zigzags and parallel lines. Photo by Robert David.

Parallel Lines

Another image group that appears in large concentrations consists of short parallel lines. Some occur in isolated rows (Figure 17), while others are combined with holes, which were drilled into the engraved lines after the lines were created (Figure 18). They range in size from just a few to more than 30 cm long. They range from groups of fewer than a dozen to groups approaching one hundred or more. The smaller variety is especially concentrated in the cave located in section 100N100W. Whether this indicates an artistic preference for the shelter walls or is an ideological variant associated specifically with the cave cannot be determined. Tally marks, as they have been called elsewhere, are common in both public and private settings. They appear with comparable frequency at Petroglyph Point and fall into Crotty's "Rectilinear Abstract" category (Crotty 1981:158).

Drilled Holes

The final class of residual markings consists of concentrations of drilled holes, which like the fields of zigzags and parallel lines appear with varied intensities all over 4-Mod-22. In some cases they appear in groupings of shallow "pock marks" that are either randomly placed or arranged in small clusters; elsewhere they are more deeply engraved and occur in groups that exceed 70. Sometimes smaller groups are enclosed within a circular or curvilinear line (Figure 19). As previously indicated, they have occasionally been drilled within the grooves of parallel lines and iconic motifs, such as the triangle previously shown in Figure 13D. On more rare occasions drilled holes comprise complete motifs in and of themselves (Figure 20).

Although other rock art sites contain cupules and indentations that are similar to those found on 4-Mod-22, holes created by drilling are known only to exist on The Peninsula and in a small cave on a hill near Tule Lake (Hann and Bettles 2006:184). At both of these locations the rock material is comprised of wielded volcanic tuft, which has the consistency of sandstone and can easily be incised using even one's fingernail. An experiment carried out by archaeologist Don Hann demonstrated that holes could be drilled into this material using an ordinary, untipped fire drill with relative ease (Hann and Bettles 2006:190). The use of a fire drill to create these holes has relevant ideological ramifications that are discussed at length in the next chapter.

Figures 17: Carved parallel lines appear either in isolated, unembellished rows or in association with other glyphs, such as the carved zigzags to the left. Photo by MaKai Magié.

Dot patterns in rock art at painted sites are especially concentrated in cave contexts but also occur at open-air sites with much less frequency (e.g., Loring and Loring 1983:19, Figure 157). It is not known if the painted varieties were intended to emulate the drilled holes that appear on The Peninsula sites. The dot patterns on nearby SIS-288 certainly show similar arrangements.

Figure 18: Engraved parallel lines filled in with drilled holes. Photo by MaKai Magié.

Figure 19: Shaman supplicants drilled holes in the rock face as a means of communicating with their spirit familiars. Photo by MaKai Magié.

Figure 20: Iconic motifs created with the use of drilled holes. Photo by MaKai Magié.

Geometric Figures

Geometric figures are difficult to detect among the other images largely because of the highly abstract nature of Klamath Basin rock art in general and because of their aforementioned synechdoche representations. Nevertheless, the geometric figures that appear below are common to rock art sites everywhere, even in the cave paintings of Paleolithic Europe (Lewis-Williams 2002:206). Those that appear on 4-Mod-22 are, by and large, isolated from the site's main rock art concentrations. But even when this was not the case, it was apparent that the artists deliberately set them apart, either by depicting them at right angles to other motifs in order to emphasize the contrast or by using different engraving techniques. The geometric figures below occur with about the same frequency as those on Petroglyph Point. While they appear in both open-air contexts and within the nearby lava tubes, they are by far more heavily concentrated in the caves (Loubser and Whitley 1999:1:73–74).

Paired Zigzags

Paired zigzags make up a relatively small percentage of the geometric figures on 4-Mod-22 (Figure 21). Distinguished from other zigzags in that they always appear in pairs, these engravings were arranged so one or more of their terminal ends interact directly with natural fractures in the rock faces that frame them. As indicated, these figures occur at Petroglyph Point and in the nearby lava tube sites, but the degree of this kind of interaction with panel face features has not yet been determined on that site. On 4-Mod-22, their direct association with fissures and cracks factors greatly in their interpretation.

Isolated Grids

Isolated grids comprise one of the smallest percentages of engravings at 4-Mod-22. Although grids may occur anywhere in Klamath Basin rock art, they are more frequently found in caves and outdoor sites in private settings. They occur with about equal frequency at Petroglyph Point. They fall into Crotty's Closed Rectilinear category (Crotty 1981:158). Given the strong rattlesnake theme apparent on this site, the diamond-pattern variety shown in Figure 22E may have been intended to represent a snake's skin patterning. But as previously indicated, without other markings indicative of snake properties, they were classified simply as geometric.

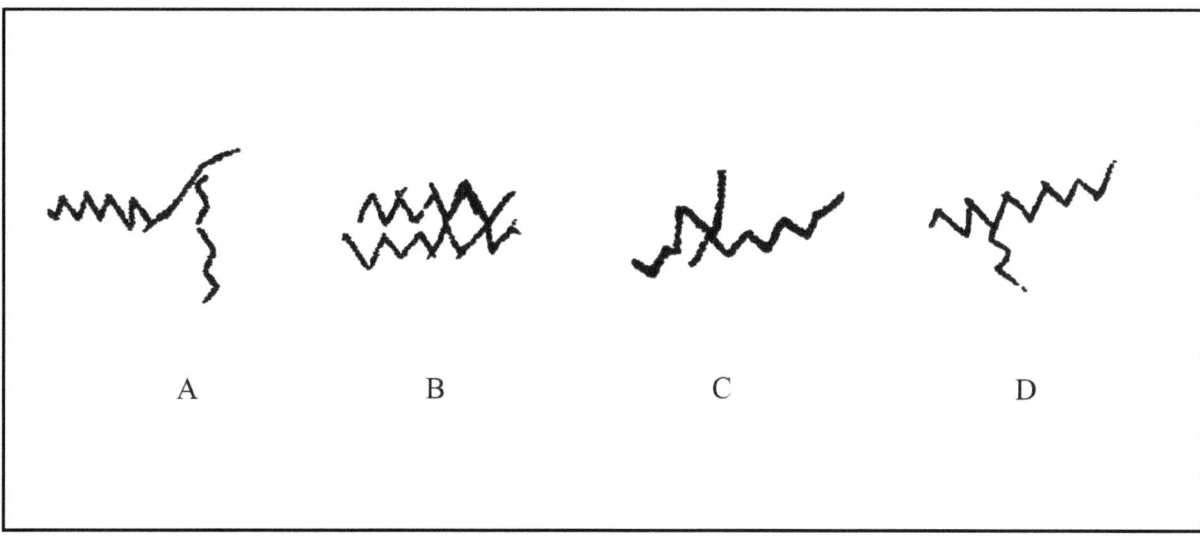

Figure 21: Paired zigzag figures from 4-mod-22. Tracings by Robert David.

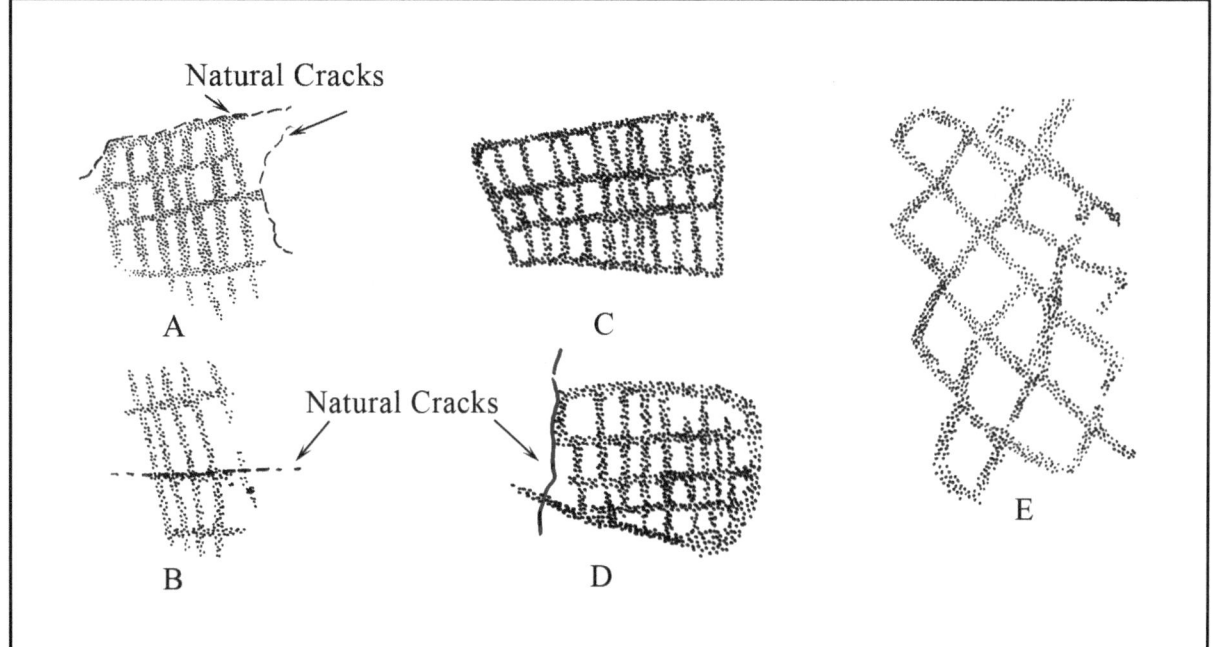

Figure 22: Sample of grid figures from 4-Mod-22. Tracings by Robert David.

Bisected Diamond and Ovoid Chains

Bisected diamond and ovoid chains are distinguished from the longer diamond- and zigzag-chain varieties in that they are vertically bisected with a straight line and are deliberately smaller and isolated from other petroglyph concentrations (Figure 23). Loubser and Whitley (1999:2:18–19, 71, 141) noted their appearance elsewhere in the Klamath Basin in three of the caves within Lava Beds National Monument, and I noted others at open-air sites, such as SIS-288 and Petroglyph Point, where they fall within Crotty's Straight and Curved Line Combinations category (Crotty 1981:158).

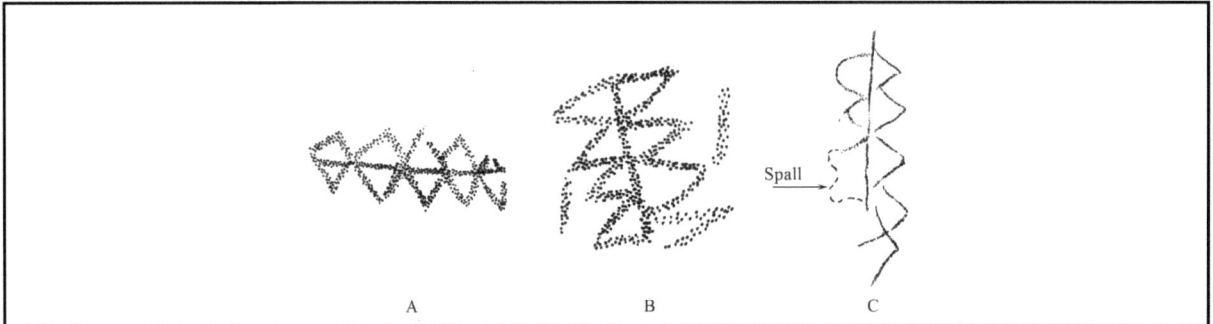

Figure 23: Bisected diamond and ovoid chains from 4-Mod-22. Tracings by Robert David.

Intersecting Lines

The three examples of intersecting lines in Figure 24 are distinguished from the skeletal figures above by their upward angled "ribs," which makes them somewhat more similar to plants than skeletons. All of the anthropomorphic figures at Petroglyph Point, as well as within the cave system at Lava Beds National Monument, are depicted with downward angled ribs—a point that played a determining role in this classification. Also, unlike the skeletal figures, these designs are all directly associated with zigzag figures at right angles, which give them the appearance of a tree standing atop a hill (see Figure 25). No similar motifs with upward angled chevrons are apparent on Petroglyph Point. In the nearby lava tube sites, however, Loubser and Whitley (1999:2:107) noted three. The first, located at the Symbol Bridge site, appears somewhat anthropomorphic but has "heads" on both the top and bottom ends. The remaining two are located within Symbol Bridge and consist of one incomplete painting that may be anthropomorphic in nature and the other a single line bisecting three upward chevrons. None of the figures in the lava tubes are associated with zigzag lines as they are at 4-Mod-22.

Combs

"Comb" or "rake" figures, as they have been called elsewhere (Keyser et al. 2004:40), are made of a single straight line with a series of parallel lines that radiate at right angles. Figures 26B and C are directly associated with the paired zigzags in section 130N100W. Figure 26A is discreetly located in section 100N100W.

Crotty noted a few of these designs engraved at Petroglyph Point, and classified them as "Intersecting Straight Lines" in her Rectilinear Abstract category (Crotty 1981:158). Many more appear in the painted variety within the nearby lava tube sites (Loubser and Whitley 1999:2:15, 50, 69, 85, 221). Although they do occasionally occur at open-air sites, they are pointedly absent from public contexts, suggesting that they may have been important specifically to the artists but not to the non-shaman public.

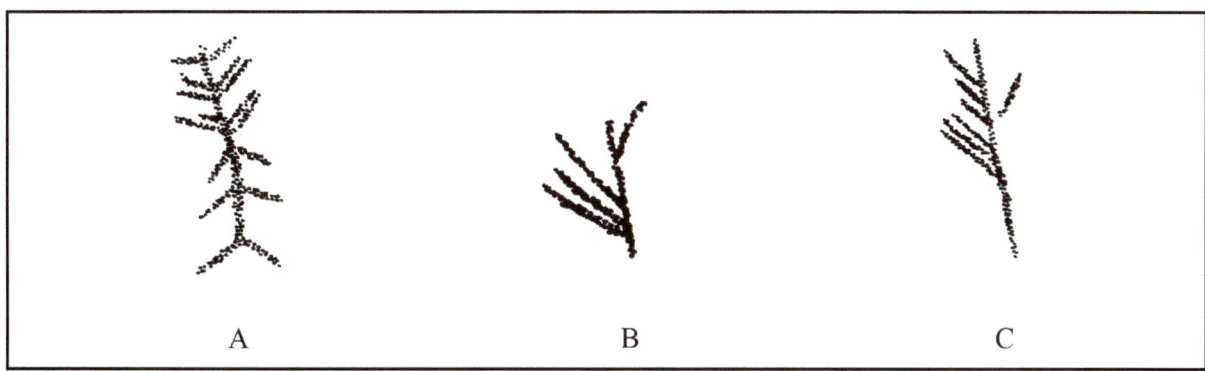

Figure 24: Intersecting lines from 4-Mod-22. Tracings by Robert David.

Figure 25: Figures that resemble plants are commonly associated with zigzags at 4-Mod-22. Photo by MaKai Magié.

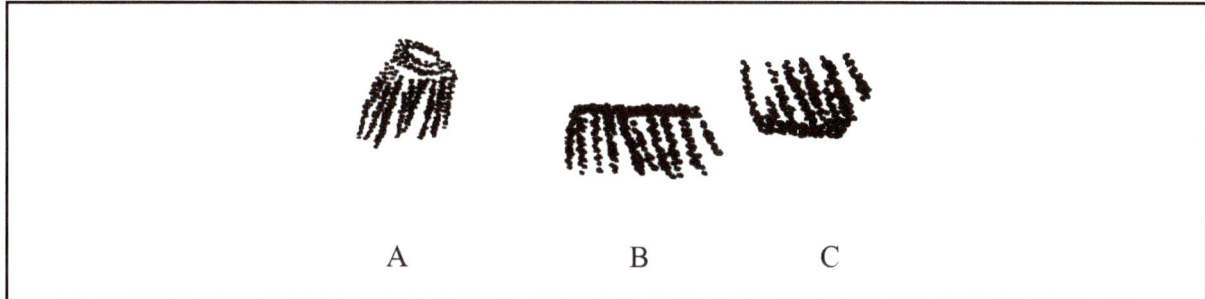

Figure 26: Sample of comb designs at 4-Mod-22. Tracings by Robert David.

Bisected Lines

Bisected lines appear only three times on 4-Mod-22. All three examples in Figure 27 are located in section 140N100W. Known elsewhere as "ladder" forms or "centipedes," these figures appear all throughout the Pacific Northwest with varying degrees of frequency. In the Klamath Basin, they are most commonly found in private settings, although a variant of this image is located in an open-air site near Klamath Marsh (Loring and Loring 1983:18, Figure 155). Crotty has also noted a few at Petroglyph Point where they appear with about the same frequency as those on 4-Mod-22 (Crotty

1981:158). Notably, however, their frequency may be higher than that presently identified. There are some instances where a series of carved lines appear to deliberately intersect natural cracks and points of cleavage on the rock face, effectively forming a very similar pattern. This must certainly be taken into consideration when future comprehensive motif counts are conducted on this site. Given the strong presence of rattlesnake referents on 4-Mod-22, it is altogether possible that bisected lines depict a "stick" version of the rattlesnake's rattles, such as that shown in Figure 11A.

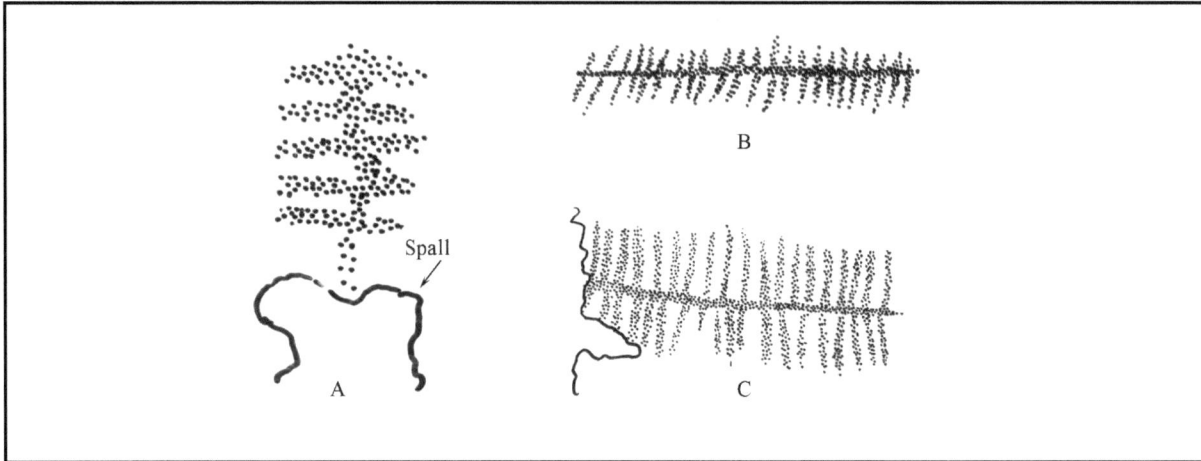

Figure 27: Sample of bisected lines from 4-Mod-22. Tracings by Robert David.

Barred Rectangles

Similar to the bisected lines, the barred rectangles in Figure 28 are concentrated on the south-central portion of 4-Mod-22 and constitute a minor presence. Figure 28A is located within Section 120N100W, while Figures 28B and C both occur in Section 140N100W.

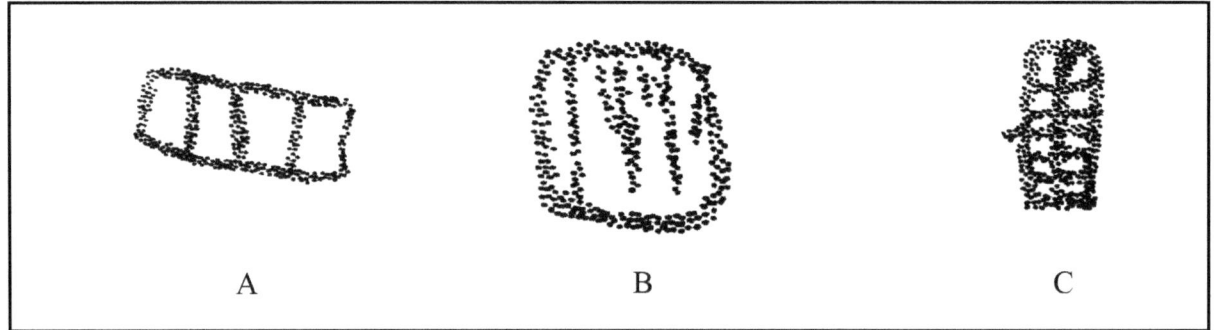

Figure 28: Sample of barred rectangles from 4-Mod-22. Tracings by Robert David.

Generally speaking, barred rectangles occur more frequently in public settings than bisected lines. This could indicate that they represent a possible iconic motif in their own right, since they may have been something people would have recognized. They are minimally represented in the nearby lava tubes, and only a few are noted at nearby Petroglyph Point (Crotty 1981:158). Like the bisected lines above, these figures may symbolize a rattlesnake's rattle, such as in Figure 11E. It is also possible, however, that the barred rectangle falls into the "grid" geometric category but is reduced to its most minimal form.

Conclusions

The rock art of 4-Mod-22 exhibits a variety of patterns and interrelationships that factor in no small way into the interpretations for this site. Iconic motifs demonstrate a strong tendency to show up in public contexts at other Klamath Basin rock art sites; their presence in other locations indicates that these motifs were both widely recognized and used by other artists. The geometric figures, by contrast, tend to show up more frequently in private settings, and in greater concentrations. Loubser and Whitley (1999:1:72) have observed that the rock paintings in some of the caves within Lava Beds National Monument are comprised completely of geometric figures. This strongly suggests that their function was more of a private matter to the artist and was not intended for public viewing or use. The fact that many of these figures are isolated from the main rock art concentrations on 4-Mod-22 is likely a reflection of their private use elsewhere.

The residual markings are more difficult to affiliate because their significance lies in the behaviors that produced them rather than the designs themselves. Most of The Peninsula rock art sites bear these markings, while others have been reported in the aforementioned cave on the east side of Tule Lake (Hann and Bettles 2006:184). Markings of this kind, however, were not limited to rock exposures comprised of wielded volcanic tuft. Spier (1930:141) described a boulder on the west side of Klamath Lake that shamans used to ritually pound with a harder stone in order to control the winds. Pounding on the south side of this rock, for example, was thought to bring a south wind. After so many generations, this pounding created rows of small cupules that lined the boulder's edges. But the apparent organization in the way these cupules were arranged was guided by the expectation of the ritual, not by a particular design envisioned by their creators.

What this demonstrates is that some categories of Klamath Basin markings were known to be by-products of ritual behaviors, and that interacting with certain rock surfaces was done in order to influence the natural order. This is very likely what is taking place at 4-Mod-22. But because they resulted from drilling rather than pounding, it is not likely that their creation had anything to do with controlling the weather. Instead, their integration with the iconic motifs indicates that they had to do with influencing the beliefs and expectations the iconic figures symbolized to the artists. I discuss this at length in the following chapter.

Chapter 4

Interpretation of 4-Mod-22 Petroglyphs

> *Rock art is a manifestation of religious belief, ritual activities, prayers to the gods and spirits, or attempts to acquire supernatural power. What is 'communicated' was never literal but spiritual. Supernatural power is basic in shamanistic societies in that all things contain power to some degree, but certain places, individuals, or objects were believed to have power in concentrated form. It was the job of the shaman to make supplications, contact the supernatural world, and safeguard the welfare of the tribe, and a natural landmark or exotic feature such as a cave or cliff would be revealed to the shaman as a place of power, and sacred rites would be enacted, often including the making of rock art.*
>
> ——Lee, Hyder, and Benson, The Rock Art of Petroglyph Point and Fern Cave, Lava Beds National Monument.

When viewed in conjunction with ethnographic and mythological texts, the three rock art categories identified on 4-Mod-22 indicate two ritual behaviors were taking place on this site. These include shamans' consultations with their spirit familiars and shamans' power quests. By spirit consultations I refer to the situation described in the quote from Gatschet below, which is recalled from Chapter 1.

> Another class of spirits embodies the spirits of those animals, which have to be consulted by the kiuks or conjurer when he is called to treat a case of disease. Such persons only who have been trained during five years for the profession of conjurers can see these spirits, but by them they are seen as clearly as we see the objects around us. To see them they have to go to the home of a deceased conjurer, and at night only. He is then led by a spirit called Yayaya-ash [sic] appearing in the form of a one-legged man towards the spot where the animal spirits live; this specter presides over them; there the conjurer notices that each appears different from the other, and is at liberty to consult them about the patient's case. Yayaya-ash means "the frightener," and by the myth-tellers is regarded as the Thunder or its spirit. (Gatschet 1890a:xcviii)

By shamans' power quests I refer to those occasions described by Ray (1963:36), when shamans returned to known spirit locales in order to refresh their relationship with their spirit familiars. The Peninsula lies at the very heart of the Klamath-Modoc world and is comprised of the original matter from which Kumush formed the earth (Ray 1963:18). One Modoc tale identifies it as a gathering place where great mythological beings met in council for five years to establish the natural order of things that would ensure a healthy balance among humans, animals, and other living things (Curtin 1884:670–681). In this light, The Peninsula can certainly be considered a place where the "animal spirits" described by Gatschet lived. As such, it is a place where shamans, under the guidance of Yahyahyaas, would certainly have visited in order to consult or renew their relationship with their spirit familiars.

Through careful application of ethnographic and mythological texts, I show that the iconic motifs represent the spirit familiars commonly used by Klamath-Modoc shamans and that residual markings are the trace markings shamans left behind in their efforts to ritually consult with these spirits by manipulating the rock face. The geometric figures, while specific to neither spirit consultations nor power quests, nonetheless denote the shamans' experiences in the supernatural world and are thus considered references to trance.

Iconic Motifs

A careful application of ethnography and myth shows that the iconic motifs on this site represent shamans' spirit familiars. These are the particular spirits that shamans call upon to diagnose sicknesses and affect cures. Depictions of these spirits on the 4-Mod-22 rock face are indicative of the shamans' belief that spirits lived within this land formation (The Peninsula) and could be accessed at this and similar rock exposures.

Circles and Sunbursts

Circles and sunbursts are among the most common motif in Klamath Basin rock art and are widely thought to represent the sun disk of Kumush, who was the Klamath and Modoc creator and spirit of the sun (Hann and Bettles 2006:187). According to myth, prior to gaining possession of the sun disk, Kumush was a shaman living on the east side of Klamath Lake where he was reputed to return people to life in his sweat lodge. One day, a grief-stricken woman brought him a bright-shining disk, which had been the clothing of her lover whom her brothers had mistakenly slain. She begged Kumush to use it to bring her lover back to life. But Kumush saw the disk's beauty and power and wanted it for himself. Instead of using it to save the woman's lover, he took the disk for himself and placed it in the small of his back, where it became a permanent part of him. Since that time, Kumush and the sun disk were one and the same (Curtin 1912:1–6).

Allied with the sun disk, Kumush harbored tremendous supernatural powers. In spite of this, however, descriptions of his deeds in the tales make it clear that he also represents all of the exaggerated flaws of human nature. At every turn he became the victim of his own pranks and misdeeds, which, often as not, resulted in his gruesome death. But no matter how horribly he was mangled and torn, Morning Star, who was the medicine of the sun disk, arrived on the scene and returned him to life: "And nothing remained except the disk. And Morning Star said to the disk, 'why do you sleep so long? Get up old man!' And he [Kumush] got up as before, and he will last as long as the disk and the morning star" (Curtin 1884:212).

The sun disk and Morning Star personify the relationship between the sun and Venus, also known as the evening and morning stars. In this relationship, the sun appears to die at night as it descends over the horizon, with the evening star following close behind. At dawn, however, the (now) morning star precedes the sunrise, thus appearing to have caught the sun and, with its return, brought it back to life. Morning Star was thus believed to be the sun disk's medicine. Because Morning Star brought the sun back to life every morning, Kumush, came to be the beneficiary of its rejuvenating power.

When he first brought people to the upper, physical world, Kumush knew that they would need supernatural assistance to help them ward off sickness and disease. Thus it was Kumush who first ordained the role of shamans. As the founder of shamanism, Kumush was every shaman's tutelary (Hann and Bettles 2006:183; Whitley et al. 2004:232). Together, with his medicines, Kumush, represented just about the most powerful spirit familiar any shaman could possess. The pervasiveness of his medicine symbol, the sun disk, in Klamath Basin rock art is a direct reflection of Kumush's importance in the shamans' ritual enterprise (Figure 29).

Figure 29: The nucleated concentric circle is the most widespread motif in Klamath Basin rock art and represents the sun, sun halo, and morning star combined into a single emblem. Photo by Robert David.

Skeletal Figures

Skeletal figures are very common in North American rock art and are widely thought to depict shamans who have died and returned to life, a common metaphor for the metaphysical journey they make between the physical and spiritual worlds through trance (Eliade 1964:63). In the Klamath-Modoc worldview, skeletal figures represent the spirit Skoks. In ethnography and myth, skoks are the souls of deceased people who have either returned from the land of the dead or that have not yet departed thereto. They are described as bones, skeletons, or skeleton-like shades with a hump on their backs and a bundle at their sides. Considered fatally dangerous, they constantly wander about at night seeking to snatch someone's soul to take to the land of the dead (Gatschet 1890a:xcvi; Ray 1963:49–50; Spier 1930:101). For this reason they were greatly feared. Shamans, however, were able to use Skoks's dangerous properties to their advantage. Because of their ability to transcend death, it was thought that any shaman who had Skoks as a spirit familiar could bring their patients back to life (Curtin 1884:624, 1912:226).

Anthropomorphic Figures

Some of the anthropomorphic figures at 4-Mod-22 represent shamans' spirit familiars, while others are very likely to be self-portraits of the shaman-artists themselves. Those that depict spirit familiars would have been consulted by shamans who made pilgrimages to the site under the guidance of Yahyahyaas; those depicting the shamans' self-portraits are typically associated with power questing and trance.

According to myth, before Kumush brought ordinary humans to the upper world, the earth was inhabited by supernatural beings very similar in appearance to the animals and humans of today (Ray 1963:18). When ordinary humans supplanted them, these "first inhabitants" were transformed into spirit beings. The most human like of these beings were called the *psaudiwas*. Along with their spirit animal counterparts, psaudiwas provided shamans with supernatural abilities. It seems only natural that depictions of psaudiwas would appear in the same places where spirit animals are also depicted. This pattern is very apparent at 4-Mod-22. As spirit familiars, psaudiwas would certainly be among those spirits shamans consulted in matters related to sickness and disease.

Some of the human representations may also depict the artists' self-portraits as they perceived themselves in altered states of consciousness. Self-portraits are common rock art motifs that are completed by power quest supplicants who wished to commemorate their personal trance experience. According to Lewis-Williams and Dowson (1988:211),

> in this climactic period, images [within the subject's mind] are fantastically combined and the subject inhabits rather than merely witnesses a bizarre hallucinatory world. We call this condition participation. . . . Some rock art depictions of human beings probably represent participation, but we must allow that it would be difficult to distinguish between images of the subject him- [or her-] self and images of other persons [they] might encounter in [this] altered state of consciousness.

Indications that The Peninsula is a location associated with shamanic power questing are found in the myths. The mythical characters Kumush and Aisis both embarked on power quests around the Klamath Basin, both using The Peninsula as their starting point. In both instances, they left their markings on the rocks at the outset of their travels (Curtin 1884:220, 255). Guided by the protocols they established, shamans, too, would have left markings on the rocks at the outset of their own power quest journeys.

Various characteristics of the anthropomorphic beings previously shown in Figure 8 support both the spirit consultations and power questing interpretations for this site. The human figures depicted with either tails or phallic elements in Figures 8E, 8G, and 8H, for example, are indicative of shamanic trance experiences (Whitley 1994, 1998). Phallic symbolism derives largely from the fact that shamans, while under trance, commonly experience erections and nocturnal emissions, which were taken by others to be evidence of shamans copulating with spirits (Devereux 1949:111; Gayton 1948:11; Lowie 1909:224–225; Whitley 1998:19). Indications from myth suggest that these sexual metaphors for shamanic trance were also active in the Klamath Basin. One Modoc tale in particular describes how Lulusdewieas, a mythical old man, painted his phallus with black paint before engaging in a sort of sexual intercourse with the lava fields (Curtin 1884:27–28). The majority of pictographs in these caves were rendered in black pigment, suggesting a connection between the old man's sexual act and the creation of the rock art. According to Whitley et al. (2004:229), this story provides a mythical justification for the location of the rock art, while at the same time the sexual symbolism denotes its trance origins.

By the same token, Figures 8E, 8G, and 8H may also represent therianthropic motifs, symbolizing a blend of human and animal traits. As was common in shamanic societies elsewhere, the actions of Klamath-Modoc shamans and their spirit familiars were indistinguishable, and thus they were considered one and the same beings. According to Spier (1930:109), "the shaman is possessed during his performances. He is the vehicle of the spirit; the spirit sings with his voice, sucks with his lips, and sees with his eyes. It is not in him at other times, but in its home in the mountains or under the water and must be called on to enter his body."

The occurrence of human figures depicted with animal characteristics served as an important metaphor for the relationship between shamans and their spirit familiars. Other indications of shamanic trance are the depictions of legless anthropomorphic beings in Figures 8I–8K that appear to denote flight. Astral projection and the sensation of weightlessness are among the many somatic metaphors associated with shamanic trance. They are often described as the "magical flight" of the shamans as they traveled to and within the supernatural world (Lewis-Williams 2001:342).

Spirit Figures

The three spirit figures identified on this site have no specific referent in the Klamath Basin ethnographic or mythological literature. A comparison with similar motifs from the Columbia Plateau demonstrates that figures of this nature are widespread. Given the importance of vision quests and spirit helpers among Plateau peoples, Keyser suggests that they may depict the artists' highly individualized perceptions of their guardian spirits (Keyser 1992:52).

The depiction in Figure 9A is directly associated with a cluster of drilled holes just above the point where its appendages cross (also see Figure 30). Figure 9B is similarly associated with a single drilled hole just below the appendages' crossing point. No residual markings, including drilled holes, are associated with Figure 9C. Nevertheless, for reasons discussed below, the direct relationship between drilled holes and some of these figures indicate that the artists regard them as having supernatural potency and revisited them subsequent to their creation. Given their slight tendency toward anthropomorphism in the 4-Mod-22 and Mod-1 assemblages, it is possible that they represent extremely stylistic depictions of psaudiwas. Without corroborating information from ethnography or myth, however, interpretations for these figures must remain speculative.

Rattlesnakes

As indicated in Figure 11, rattlesnake depictions at 4-Mod-22 exhibit a variety of stylistic representations. According to Ray (1963:46), every shaman possessed the Rattlesnake Spirit as a medicine. Figure 11E depicts a rattlesnake's exaggerated rattle and a curious grid design scratched above that probably symbolizes the snake's skin, both of which were considered to be especially powerful. The rattle was believed to produce thunder, while its skin had various curative properties (Spier 1930:119, 129). Shamans, in fact, kept their curing pipes wrapped in a rattlesnake's skin, probably to enhance their pipe's supernatural properties (Curtin 1884:677; Spier 1930:87–88). That the Rattlesnake's rattle was said to summon Thunder might, in fact, be a reference to Yahyahyaas, who himself personified Thunder's spirit (Gatschet 1890a:xcviii). Not only did Yahyahyaas preside over spirit consultations, he himself was also a spirit in his own right. Depictions of the snake's rattles may have been intended to summon Yahyahyaas himself.

Figure 30: Drilled holes associated with this spirit figure indicate that prehistoric shamans consulted with the spirit it was believed to depict. Photo by MaKai Magié.

Although the snake image in Figure 11D from the table closely resembles that in Figure 11A, it does not possess a rattle. This raises the possibility that it was not intended to depict Rattlesnake Spirit. While it is entirely possible that the artist simply chose not to include a rattle, snakes of all kinds, in fact, were considered spiritually potent. Because they shed their skins, they were thought to possess regenerative properties that made them immortal (Ray 1963:25). By way of analogy, shamans would use these regenerative properties to cure their patients. It is difficult to imagine that other snakes would be excluded from appearing in the rock art.

Snake and rattlesnake depictions on this site thus denote shamans' consultations or shamanic trance in the form of his or her spirit helper, but a third possibility is that they are indications of sorcery. By "sorcery" I refer to shamans' use of their spirit familiars to assassinate enemies at a distance. Like any other spirit in the shamans' pantheon, Rattlesnake Spirit could be used to heal or to harm. One story tells of how a weak and sickly son of a chief became a powerful shaman overnight after visiting Rattlesnake Spirit and his daughters in their lodge beneath Klamath Lake (Curtin 1884:73–74). But another story describes how Old Snake (a rattlesnake) succumbed to his temptation to release sickness into the world. As he contemplated his decision, he smoked Indian tobacco and sang incantations "like a doctor" (Curtin 1884:450–453). Though less commonly spoken of, sorcery was another shamanic function in which rock art may have played a role (Gatschet 1890b:135; Loubser and Whitley 1999:1:63). One famous Modoc shaman, Jakalunas, was reputed to have been especially successful at doing this (Ray 1963:68–69). In this light, the story of Old Snake suggests that the Rattlesnake Spirit may have been a necessary element in rituals of this kind.

Triangular Figures

Based on information provided by Gatschet (1890a:ci–cii) and Curtin (1884, 1912), I have proposed elsewhere that triangular figures in Klamath-Modoc rock art represent the mythical character Tskel, the pine marten (David 2012a:80–82), which is a well-known shamans' medicine spirit in the Klamath Basin (Gatschet 1890a:xxxii–xxxiii, 168).

Figure 31: The North American pine marten is characterized by its elongated body and triangular head. Photo downloaded from https://commons.wikimedia.org/wiki/File%3AMarten_with_Flowers.jpg.

The North American pine marten is a long, slender-bodied weasel that has a characteristic triangular head and sharp nose (see Figure 31). As previously shown in Figure 14, its long body and triangular head are the traits most commonly featured in Klamath Basin rock art. On this site, the head alone has been emphasized, albeit with some minor variations. The most notable of these is shown in Figure 13D. After the artist had carved out the typical triangular shape in the rock face, a series of drilled holes was subsequently superimposed. The reasons for this arrangement will be discussed below.

Identified ethnographically as a shaman's medicine spirit, Tskel ruled over the Klamath Marsh country and lived near the Yamsay River (Clark 1953:56; Gatschet 1890a:ci). In myth, he possessed a medicine stick that he carried behind his ear, which he used to cure the sick, even to the point of returning them to life (Curtin 1912:326, 330). Like other medicine spirits, Tskel not only affected cures, he also acted as a shaman's servant in which he scouted the landscape for malicious spirits thought to have been bringing disease and sickness into the village (Gatschet 1890a:154, 159). As an important mythological being and shaman's spirit helper, Tskel's image would certainly appear in Klamath Basin rock art.

Iconic Motifs Conclusions

Through the application of myth it is possible to identify many of the iconic motifs on 4-Mod-22 as shamans' spirit familiars. The appearance of so many of these figures indicates that shamans believed that these spirits lived within The Peninsula itself. Evidence for nearby power questing activities in the lava fields, along with the known use of Indian tobacco to induce trance, suggests that these motifs probably derived from visions experienced during altered states of consciousness. On a larger scale, rock art sites around the whole Peninsula host hundreds if not thousands of such motifs and this land formation may be thought of as a repository for shamans' medicines. Shamans would have returned to these depictions from time to time to consult with their spirits in matters related to curing. As Gatschet has indicated, they would have done this at night under the guidance of Yahyahyaas (Gatschet 1890a:xcviii).

The method with which shamans consulted these spirits left trace markings that can be seen all over the site either in isolated groups or directly associated with particular iconic motifs that represented their spirit familiars. In the following section I discuss residual markings and explain why they denote shamans' communication with their spirits.

Residual Markings

Residual markings are the glyphs shamans made in their efforts to communicate with their spirit familiars. The tedious and repetitive motions required to create them were analogous to the labor-intensive tasks associated with the ordinary power quest, a point also noted in part by Lee et al. (1988:137). The markings that fall into this image category include zigzag concentrations, groups of parallel lines, and concentrations of drilled holes. Unlike other petroglyphs on the site, these were created randomly, often in large concentrations, and intimately associated with the iconic motifs described before. Their relationship with the iconic motifs factors significantly in the interpretations proposed for this site.

Although identical markings are also located at rock art sites in public settings, such as villages and large camps, they are more common and occur in significantly larger concentrations in private settings where shamans would have gone to consult with or renew their relationships with their spirit familiars. One such location is east of Tule Lake. Ethnographic informants identified it as a shaman's cave and said it was inhabited by ghosts ([e.g., spirits] Riddle 1890; Whitley et al. 2004:231). The markings all around and inside this cave are comprised of the same zigzags, scratched lines, and drilled holes found at 4-Mod-22 and nearby Petroglyph Point. According to Hann and Bettles (2006:184), these markings were made by Kumush as he carved out a window through which he could periodically check on his creation.

Markings of this nature are fairly common in far western North America and have good ethnographic documentation. Similar to the residual markings at 4-Mod-22, the engravings identified as the Columbia Plateau Scratched style, first classified by Keyser and Taylor (2002), often occur on rock faces containing other glyphs but appear most frequently as random incisions. Sometimes, however, they combine to form recognizable motifs of their own just as they do on 4-Mod-22. Those that do are primarily of the geometric variety, but a very rare few also form naturalistic representations ([e.g., iconic motifs] Keyser and Taylor 2006:203).

According to Keyser and Taylor (2006:211) these incisions are affiliated with an impressive form of ritual behavior in which shaman supplicants would ritually gash themselves in order to gain contact with their spirits. Columbia Plateau people thought of the human body as a container for supernatural power, and they could release this power in the form of blood through ritual gashing. In a similar fashion, certain rocks were also thought to contain supernatural power, and like ritual gashing, this power could be released by scratching the face of these rocks (Keyser and Taylor 2006:217–219). Creating particular designs, either on the body or the rock face, though sometimes done, was not a necessary part of this ritual procedure (Figure 32).

Figure 32: Columbia Plateau shamans ritually gashed certain rocks to release the supernatural power contained therein. Photo courtesy of Mike W. Taylor.

In a similar fashion, supplicants elsewhere in western North America would scratch or pound on special rocks in order to generate rock chips, which they would then grind up into a fine powder for ritual use. Like blood, the rock powder was believed to contain the rock's supernatural potency. Found throughout California, the markings generated by these behaviors fall into David Whitley's Far Western Pit and Groove Tradition (Figure 33), and are very similar to those of the Columbia Plateau Scratched style (Keyser and Taylor 2006:217). They were founded on the belief that rocks were entrances into the supernatural world and thus were places where power could be obtained. The ethnographic record for this region indicates that the Pit and Groove Tradition was related to female fertility. To guarantee conception, a woman would use a phallic-shaped pestle to grind or peck small cups into the rock and then place the resulting powder (which symbolized the supernatural power in the rocks) into her vagina just before coitus (Whitley 2000:98).

In the Klamath Basin, shamans created similar markings on boulders using pestles, which they would repeatedly pound in order to control the direction of the wind. Rhythmically pounding certain sides of the rock was believed to generate a wind from that direction (Spier 1930:21, 141). Although the cupules resulting from this activity tended to form neat rows along the edges of the boulders (Figure 34), this arrangement was dictated by ritual necessity rather than the artists' intent to create a composition.

What these examples demonstrate is that there exists a widespread practice of creating markings on rocks in order to release or control the supernatural power believed to reside within them. This includes the Klamath Basin. At site 4-Mod-22, and at Petroglyph Point, these markings are indicative of the shamans' intent to consult with their spirit familiars. Ritually scratching or drilling

Figure 33: The rock powder resulting from these scratches and cupules (Pit and Groove) was thought to enhance female fertility among some Native Californian peoples. Photo adapted from Whitley (2000:49, Figure 34) with author's permission.

Figure 34: Cupules situated around the edges of "rain rocks" were generated to control the direction of the wind. Photo by Robert David.

into the rock face was a means of entering the supernatural world. The heavy association between residual markings and iconic motifs, which have been shown to represent shamans' spirits, indicate that the ritual scratching and drilling were directed at these spirit beings. In some cases, prehistoric artists drilled patterns of holes directly into iconic engravings in order to consult directly with the spirits they represented (e.g., Figure 13D). It should be remembered, however, that the whole rock face was thought to be the "house" for these spirit beings, and in light of this, residual markings were placed either randomly or in varying concentrations on the cliff face whether or not iconic symbols were present. Simply drilling into the rock or engraving concentrations of zigzags or parallel lines was sufficient to make contact with these spirits.

Zigzag Concentrations

The zigzag concentrations identified as residual markings differ from the paired zigzags described below in that they are comparatively pervasive on the site and appear in much larger concentrations. While it is apparent that these markings were intended to be zigzags, as opposed to random scratches, their primary goal was served in the act of engraving the rock with intensity somewhat in the nature of a power quest—a point noted earlier by Lee et al. (1988:137). The final zigzag designs were likely inspired by the belief that the spirit Yahyahyaas guided the shaman-artists to the site in order to consult with their spirit familiars (Gatschet 1890a:xcviii). In this light, creating zigzags was done somewhat in the manner of parishioners who symbolically cross themselves as they offer up their prayers. Although the motions involved in crossing themselves are not mentioned in the prayers, they do give them a sense of direction and focus. Similarly, carving these figures in such an intensive and repeated fashion was instrumental in calling and communicating with spirits because it was a way of achieving a trance-like state. As the spirit of Thunder, Yahyahyaas wielded Thunder's weapon, Lightning (Gatschet 1890a:xc), and it is in this we find an especially important clue. Lightning was a spirit figure in and of itself. According to Ray (1963:56), the Lightning was instrumental in the shamans' ability to diagnose causes of sickness. Because Lightning could light up even the night sky, it was among the first spirits called in a curing séance. The illumination provided by this spirit metaphorically made visible the unseen and unknown. By way of extending this metaphor, Lightning also enabled shamans to see their spirit familiars at 4-Mod-22. The trance-like state resulting from carving so many of these symbols would have been considerably enhanced if stacking rocks in the nearby lava fields and using Indian tobacco were also part of their ritual process. Both of these activities have been associated with calling spirits (Curtin 1884:387; Gatschet 1890a:167, 180; Spier 1930:95,127).

In this regard, carving residual markings on the rock face assisted shamans in achieving a directed state of trance. Carving them in the shape of zigzags gave their supplications a sense of focus that was perfectly compatible with their beliefs that Yahyahyaas, through the use of his weapon Lightning, would make their spirit familiars visible and accessible.

Parallel Lines

Carving parallel lines into the rock face to communicate with the supernatural world also has its precedent in myth. Two of the mythic tales collected by Curtin, in particular, associate scratching the rock face with shamanic spirit questing. In the first story, the daughters of Yaulilik climbed to the top of a mountain near Tule Lake to the lodge of Kumush and Aisis in search of a husband.[5] The fact that they carried along their bone head scratchers on their quest indicates that they were on a power quest, since this item was only used for this purpose (Spier 1930:95).

Because he was the greatest hunter in the world, the sisters desired to "marry" Aisis. Kumush however, jealous of his step son's youth, tried to trick Yaulilik's daughters into believing that he himself was Aisis so he could take them as wives for himself. Soon, however, they discovered his deceit and angrily scratched the flesh from his face with their head scratchers. In retaliation for this, Aisis killed the sisters, but after they had returned to life in a sweat lodge, they sought him out again. Soon they found him dying on a mountain and saved his life, and in so doing became his wives (Curtin 1912:35).

In the second tale, Kumush had finished creating the world and all living things and was preparing to hibernate beneath his mountain near Tule Lake (e.g., The Peninsula). Before retiring, however, he gouged out a window in the rock face with his fingernails so he could look out upon his creation and check on his people from time to time. Once this was completed, he descended to his "den" and went to sleep. He sleeps there still (Marriott and Rachlin 1968:44–46).

What is common to both of these stories is that they take place at known rock art sites, where carvings of just this nature are located. The first is a small cave on a nearby hill that has been ethnographically identified as the lodge of Kumush and Aisis and also as a shamans' power questing site (Hann and Bettles 2006:184). Scratching lines in the rock face are thus equated with ritually seeking contact with spirits. Shamans would certainly have emulated the actions of Yaulilik's daughters in the tale, knowing that the ritual procedure they used, encoded in the myth, resulted in the acquisition of their desired spirit helper, Aisis. Because the sisters were on a power quest, fasting and rock stacking are implied elements of the story. Shamans would certainly have fasted and stacked rocks prior to scratching the rock face on their own quests as did Yaulilik's daughters.

The second, of course, is that scratched lines are pervasive at all of the petroglyph sites on The Peninsula, with particular emphasis on Mod-1 (Petroglyph Point) and 4-Mod-22. Scratching the rock's surface was predicated on Kumush's desire to peer into the mortal world. By virtue of symbolic inversion, in which behaviors in the physical world were reversed from those in the spirit world (Spier 1930:102), shamans would have scratched the rock face in order to peer into the supernatural world where Kumush slept and other spirit beings lived.

At 4-Mod-22, these markings appear either in isolated concentrations or are associated with iconic motifs or other residual markings (e.g., zigzags and drilled holes). While those that are associated with particular iconic motifs indicate that the shaman-artists directly consulted specific spirits, those that are isolated from other motifs reflect the general belief that spirits lived within these rocks and could be accessed simply by penetrating the rock face, whether or not iconic motifs were present. Scratched lines that appear in conjunction with other residual markings, such as drilled holes, indicate that the supplicants used multiple techniques to consult with their spirit familiars (e.g., Figure 17).

Drilled Holes

Drilled holes are among the most conspicuous markings on the site, probably because they were created using an entirely different rendering technique and because they appear everywhere and in every conceivable arrangement. All of these arrangements are consistent with the belief that spirits dwelled within these rocks—a point previously noted by Lee et al. (1988:139).

There is little doubt that cupules are associated with power. Found throughout the world, they tend to be located near lakes, springs, waterfalls, and mountains. The very act of making [them] would imbue the supplicant with power (Younger 1974) for, by making a cupule, the maker releases power that is held within the rock by spirit beings living inside.

On 4-Mod-22, drilled holes appearing randomly or in isolated clusters are reflections of the artists' belief that spirits lived within the rock and could be accessed at any part of it. Although it was certainly done, drilling near or upon iconic motifs was not necessary for accessing them. The holes that are closely associated with iconic motifs probably depict the artist's attempt to communicate with the spirits that the iconic motifs symbolized. In a similar fashion, drilled holes arranged to depict iconic motifs themselves, like those in Figure 20, are also indicative of shamans' attempts to consult with those particular spirits. In this case, however, they incorporated the image of the spirit they sought directly into their consultation method.

Drilling holes perhaps best exemplifies the logic that guided the prehistoric shamans' belief that any of these techniques would result in an encounter with spirits. Their logic, in fact, was grounded in the ordinary power quest. During this ritual procedure, supplicants gained access to the supernatural world by engaging in a number of strenuous but economically worthless activities (Ray 1963:77). Engaging in these activities on an empty stomach and in a state of prolonged isolation resulted in trance-like dreams in which spirits appeared (Ray 1963:77; Spier 1930:95). At play in this procedure was the sense of inversion that governed how the spiritual and physical worlds were ordered. Everything in the supernatural world worked in direct opposition to that in the physical world (Spier 1930:102). Along these lines, engaging in a series of practical behaviors, such as gathering seeds or catching fish, was intended, of course, to feed the body. But engaging in economically worthless activities in which the only physical rewards were hunger and exhaustion nurtured the spirit. In this regard, attempting to create a fire by drilling holes into the rock face is an overtly meaningless pursuit unless it was done in a context of the power quest, where an engagement with spirits was sought. Like the zigzags and parallel lines, drilling holes into the rock face was intended to encourage a state of trance under which supplicants could communicate with their spirit familiars.

As a means for communicating with spirits, using a fire drill has its precedent in myth. One tale in particular describes how the leader of a group of hunters was attempting to start a fire on the mountain where he and his companions were preparing to hunt. As he turned his fire drill, he called out to the spirits and asked them for luck. To his dismay, and to that of his fellow hunters, his drilling attracted the attention of Yahyahyaas, whom they were not prepared to meet. Upon his approach, Yahyahyaas demanded tobacco and fire, as was his custom. When the hunters failed to accommodate him, Yahyahyaas killed them all (Curtin 1912:153–158).

In this tale, the most notable connection between drilled holes and talking to spirits is that the lead hunter's use of the fire drill attracted the attention of Yahyahyaas, the same spirit believed to preside over shamans' consultations at spirit abodes. It is also no small point to mention that turning the fire drill enabled the leader to talk to other spirits as well.

Another piece of information supporting this notion comes from an ethnohistoric account by Claudia Lorenz, the young daughter of a Yainax Sub-Agency employee who was stationed on the early Klamath Indian Reservation. Playing in the mountains near the sub-agency, young Claudia and her Indian playmates encountered "prayer holes" in the rocks, some of which had been painted over in red. Curious, she asked her playmates what the markings meant. They replied "that is where they talk to the Spirits" (Lorenz 1969:110).

Residual Markings Conclusions

Attempting to communicate with spirits using any of the trance-inducing methods described in this section was not done in isolation. Evidence from myth suggests that at least some of the stacked-rock features in the nearby lava fields resulted from shamans' power quests as they emulated the behaviors of Aisis and Kumush who themselves engaged in power quests (Curtin 1884:217–220, 255). Similar markings in other regions were generated by people who believed that certain rocks contained supernatural power that they could access by penetrating the rock face (Keyser and Taylor 2006:214; Whitley 2000:98–101). In this light, the Klamath Basin materials represent a localized variation of a wider-ranging perception of the supernatural world and how it operated. Among some Columbia River groups, shaman supplicants ritually gashed existing motifs in order to release the supernatural powers they contained, just as local artists did on 4-Mod-22 (Keyser and Taylor 2006:220). Some of the markings described in the final section below indicate that smoking Indian tobacco was also an important part of this process and was probably accompanied by ritual singing. When taken all together, these activities formed an elaborate and highly animated ritual process that helped shaman supplicants to approach and consult with the supernatural world.

Geometric Figures

Geometric figures consist of clusters of straight and curvilinear lines arranged to form images that today are not recognizable as objects or beings in the natural world. Throughout the world, they are thought to represent the entoptic phenomena people witness during altered states of consciousness (Lewis-Williams and Dowson 1988:203, 206) and are thus associated with shamanism. Grids, zigzags, and meandering lines are among the most common of these figures and appear on both 4-Mod-22 and Petroglyph Point in similar frequencies. Given the importance of the power quest among the Klamath and Modoc, it is likely that geometric figures are depictions of their trance experiences.

Paired Zigzags

Paired zigzags are distinguished from the zigzag concentrations previously noted in that they are much smaller and were positioned so that their terminal ends directly articulate with fissures and cracks in the rock face. This kind of interaction between imagery and the host rock is common in rock art of the North American far west and has been shown to occur in places where the rocks were believed to be portals to the supernatural world (Keyser and Poetschat 2004:128; Whitley 1998:16–17). Zigzags and wavy lines in general are among the more common entoptic figures that subjects reported witnessing during altered states of consciousness (e.g., see Figure 4). Probably because of the zigzag's resemblance to lightning, it became synonymous with a person's ability to see into the supernatural world. In the Klamath Basin, the spirit Lightning personified this very concept. It is therefore tempting to associate these figures with the Spirit Lightning, whose primary role was to provide the kind of illumination that allowed shamans to see spirits (Ray 1963:56).

Their articulation with cracks and fissures in the rock face may thus be considered references to the shamans' ability to "see" within the rocks, where spirits were believed to live.

Bisected Diamond and Ovoid Chains

While it is tempting to affiliate the bisected diamond and ovoid chains (shown in Figure 23) with entoptic phenomena, intriguing information from myth suggests that they may, in fact, symbolize Indian tobacco (*Nicotiana attenuata*). The use of Indian tobacco among the Klamath and Modoc is ethnographically associated with trance, calling spirits, and curing séances, all of which fall soundly within the role of the shamans (Curtin 1884:387; Gatschet 1890a:167, 180; Spier 1930:127). The figures on 4-Mod-22 are very similar to the tracing by Loubser and Whitley (1999:2:145) of a pictograph located at the Symbol Bridge site in Figure 35, which in turn closely compares with the photograph of the local Indian tobacco plant in Figure 36.

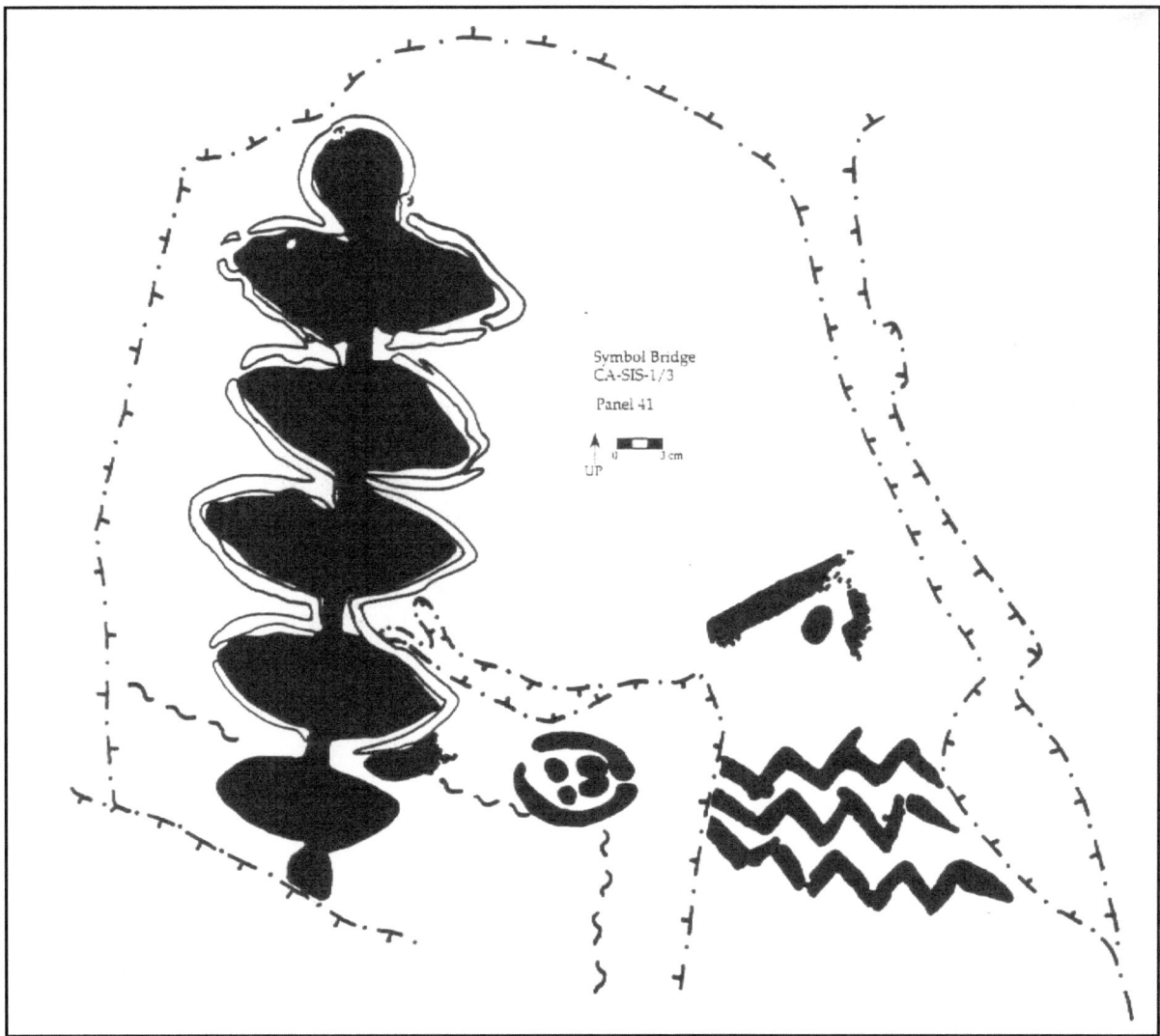

Figure 35: This figure from the Symbol Bridge site within Lava Beds National Monument resembles Indian tobacco and thus refers to the artist's own trance experience. Reproduced from Loubser and Whitley (1999:2:145). Panel 41 reproduced by permission of David S. Whitley.

Figure 36: Indian tobacco is indigenous to Northern California and was collected historically within Lava beds National Monument. Image downloaded from https://en.wikipedia.org/wiki/Nicotiana_attenuata#/media/File:Nicotiana_attenuata_in_Utah.JPG.

Ritual smoking was a widespread custom among most western North American Indian groups and was considered to be life-sustaining food for spirits (Curtin 1884; Hann 2012:106; Keyser et al. 2006:16–17; Whitley 2000:77–78; Winter 2000:308). Curtin, in fact, documented a multiple-day ceremony in which a Klamath shaman called his spirits to the winter village by consuming great quantities of tobacco (Curtin 1884, cited in Hann 2012:106). This association with tobacco and calling spirits makes the appearance of this substance in rock art seem almost inevitable.

In the mythic tales of the Klamath and Modoc, the spirit Yahyahyaas always demanded tobacco from those whom he encountered. Not providing him with tobacco was considered dangerous to the point of fatality (Curtin 1912:154, 1884:468). When one considers how strongly Yahyahyaas is implicated in relation to 4-Mod-22, depictions of Indian tobacco in the rock art might be thought of as shamans' supplications to this spirit, as prescribed in myth.

Intersecting Lines

Intersecting lines are distinguished from the skeletal figures described prior in that their ribs angle downward rather than upward. Whether this distinction is culturally significant remains to be seen. Lacking more precise ethnographic or mythological input, interpretations for this image type must remain open. It may be that they represent a stylistic variant of the suspected tobacco motifs described above. By the same token, however, the spirit Skoks was said to have been able to assume any living form, including tule grass (Curtin 1884:612). The plant-like appearance of this motif may thus be a reference to Skoks. Deur (2008:196) proposed another possibility that similar engravings at Petroglyph Point are reminiscent of lodgepole pine trees silhouetted on mountain tops. By virtue of analogy, these depictions serve as metaphors for power quest rituals that otherwise took place in the mountains. I find this explanation unlikely, however, given that shamans sought spirit power in low places on the landscape where they also depicted their art (Ray 1963:33; Whitley et al. 2004:223). High locations were typically used by non-shamans who did not make rock art. Lay persons who wished or needed to embark on a power quest would simply have gone to the mountains as ritual protocol required (Ray 1963:77; Spier 1930:95).

Curiously, the image shown as Figure 24A is comprised both of anthropomorphic and plant-like characteristics. Similar motifs, identified in extant mythologies as "tobacco people," have been observed in the Lower Columbia River drainage and ethnographically associated with shamanic trance (Hann 2012:104–105). Tobacco was certainly traded along these routes, and the ritual use of Indian tobacco in the North American far west has been widely noted

(Curtin 1884; Keyser et al. 2006:16–17; Whitley 2000:77–79; Winter 2000). It is tempting to speculate that a shaman entered into trance through the use of Indian tobacco on this site and that this combined image commemorated that experience. Without further information, however, interpretations for these figures must remain speculative.

Combs

Comb designs constitute a very minor presence in the 4-Mod-22 petroglyph assemblage. Nevertheless, they are very distinct and are found in similar proportions at Petroglyph Point and within the nearby lava tube sites. While these figures could well fit within the "grid" category described below, there is some suggestion that they may also literally symbolize shamans' combs.

Various mythical accounts describe scenarios in which shamans prepared to depart on a journey. Before leaving, however, they placed their wooden combs in the lodge rafters and told the other occupants that if the comb were to fall then that would indicate that they had been killed (Curtin 1884:76, 157, 209). Common themes in these stories include shamans, omens of death, and the resurrection of the shamans in the form of different personages.

Death is a widely used metaphor for shamanic trance in the North American far west, since only through symbolic death can shamans transcend the boundaries between the physical and supernatural worlds (Whitley 1994:13). The falling comb, in this case, would be synonymous with the shamans' successful supernatural journey. Entoptic phenomena, generated by trance and governed by the principles of perception, would certainly generate images that supplicants might perceive as objects falling, flying, or even spinning. That these figures are reminiscent of objects witnessed during the first stages of altered states of consciousness (shown in Figure 4), and that they appear at other Klamath Basin rock art sites considered to be "trance" contexts, (Loubser and Whitley 1999:2:15, 69, 85, 116, 221) adds support to this possibility.

Grids, Bisected Lines, and Barred Rectangles

Grids, bisected lines, and barred rectangles have no particular referent in Klamath-Modoc ethnography or myth. They are situated on relatively isolated parts of the rock face and make up a comparatively minor percentage of the 4-Mod-22 petroglyph assemblage. In the Klamath Basin and elsewhere, figures like this occur most commonly in private contexts where shamanic trance was known to occur, thus adding to the likelihood that they are depictions of supernatural experiences (David 2012a:117–119; Keyser 1992:93, 98, 100; Keyser et al. 2004:52–53; Lewis-Williams and Dowson 1988:205; Loubser and Whitley 1999:1:73; Whitley 1994:8–12, 2000:106–107). As a former gathering place of mythological beings, The Peninsula is certainly among the places where shamans would go to seek out these supernatural encounters.

Geometric Figures Conclusion

The geometric figures in the 4-Mod-22 rock art assemblage are distinguished by their relative isolation from the other figure types and by their abstract nature. They are strongly reminiscent of the entoptic phenomena associated with altered states of consciousness and are thus indicative of shamanic trance. Given the function proposed for this site, figures of this variety were expected to occur.

The "illumination" implicated by the paired zigzags and depictions of Indian tobacco, coupled with the "death" metaphors associated with the shamans' falling combs, support the notion that shamans carried out power quest rituals on this site that resulted in trances. Other geometric figures, such as grids, bisected lines, and barred rectangles, may be thought of as the entoptic visions shamans witnessed during their trance experiences and may, in fact, symbolize Kumush's "writing" as he embarked on a power quest journey of his own, which began from The Peninsula (Curtin 1884:255). Shamans, acting under the power of their tutelary spirit, Kumush, would certainly have recorded their visionary experiences in the same fashion (Hann et al. 2010:4; Keyser 1992:47). This is perhaps what led Spier's informants to report that Kemu'kumps made Klamath Basin rock art. *As Kemu'kumps,* shamans "wrote" their visionary experiences on the rocks.

Enhanced Natural Features

In addition to the spirit depictions on this site, there are a few naturally occurring anomalies in the rock face that resemble iconic forms that the shaman-artists enhanced with their own engravings. The two most obvious of these are the fish-like feature in section 130N100W (Figure 37) and the human-like face from section100N100W (Figure 38). In the first instance, the artist noted the natural fish shape created by irregularities in the rock face and carved over it using a series of parallel lines in much the same manner of spirit consultations. In the second instance, the artist recognized the presence of a crude, naturally formed human "face" on the rock's surface and completed the picture by adding hair, again in the form of carved parallel lines.

Figure 37: A Natural fish-like rock formation has been enhanced to complete the image and then scratched over to "communicate" with this spirit, which is probably Skoks. Photo by MaKai Magié.

Figure 38: The suggestion of a face created by natural irregularities in the rock surface prompted prehistoric artists to complete the depiction by adding hair. Photo by MaKai Magié.

The use of repeated lines to enhance these features appeals to this site's ritual philosophy in two significant ways. First, it seems to confirm the premise that spirit beings lived within these rocks. Various rock formations around the Klamath Basin were believed to be the remnants of mythical beings transformed to stone by Crow's laughter (Spier 1930:100). Thus, recognizing natural formations as spiritual beings is a well-integrated concept within Klamath-Modoc cosmology. The second involves the use of engraved parallel lines to enhance these naturally occurring features. As indicated above, these markings were used to tap into the supernatural properties believed to exist within the rock. That the artists carved parallel lines in association with each of these anomalies strongly suggests that they believed these features, too, depicted supernatural beings.

Identifying these features with specific spirit beings is fraught with the same challenges associated with any other rock art depiction. However, when we turn to ethnography and myth, it is possible to propose some promising candidates. The first derives from an ethnographic statement Klamath tribal member Dave Hill made to Albert Gatschet. Mr. Hill reported that the spirit Skoks sometimes inhabited the bodies of living fish (Gatschet 1890a:130). This might explain the enhanced fish-shaped anomaly in Figure 37. Skoks are certainly among the more powerful spirit beings in Klamath-Modoc cosmology and are represented on this site in other forms, most of which are skeletal.

The second figure (Figure 38) is more difficult to identify, since human figures could represent either psaudiwas or the artists as they perceived themselves in altered states of consciousness

(Lewis-Williams 2001:339). There is simply no way to detect the difference without consulting the artists themselves. A third possibility is that this figure may represent Yahyahyaas himself, who myth describes as having bushy hair—something that certainly set him apart from the long, straight hair style observed by both women and men among the Klamath and Modoc (Ray 1963:172; Spier 1930:213–214). In any case, what these enhancements demonstrate is that the anomalies with which they were associated motivated the artist to interact with them in a way that is consistent with the consultation markings on other parts of this site.

Panel Face Interaction

Another indication that spirits lived within The Peninsula involves how these motifs were depicted on the rock face. A close look at many of them reveals that they were not randomly placed but were instead arranged to show intentional interaction with some of the rock's natural features. This is a common practice in North American rock art, as well as in rock art around the world. One example from the Columbia River succinctly exemplifies this kind of interaction. Known locally as the half-in-half spirit figure, the anthropomorphic being in Figure 39 was painted in such a way that the white mineral stains running down the rock face perfectly bisects it, so that half appears within the stain and half on the bare gray-black rock face. At the same time, the legs and feet were painted directly above and parallel to a horizontal buckle in the rock, giving the figure the appearance of sitting atop this horizontal frame. The peoples of the Columbia Plateau believed that spirit beings lived within the rocks and functioned as shamans' spirit helpers. Local ethnography tells how shamans were considered to be very powerful and that a common metaphor is that they occupied two worlds, both the physical and spiritual, just as their spirit helpers did. This figure, according to Keyser and Poetschat (2004:127–128), very strikingly portrays a shaman, in the guise of his spirit helper, appearing simultaneously in two worlds with the spirit world implicated by the white mineral stains, and the physical world by the bare gray-black rock.

Another prehistoric example from Altamira Cave in Spain (Figure 40) is the famous bison painting depicted in the fetal position. In this painting, the artists exploited the natural contours of the cave ceiling to give their subject a sense of depth. The entire lower half of the motif follows the rock's natural features completely, suggesting that these features themselves inspired both the subject matter and its configuration. What these examples demonstrate is that the rock face was not merely a neutral backdrop for the art, but rather it served an important purpose that enabled prehistoric artists to enhance their intended messages. In essence, the rock face was every bit as important as the artwork itself. This is because the rock was considered to be the environment within which these spiritual beings lived (Keyser and Poetschat 2004:125; Spier 1930:98).

The first example from the 4-Mod-22 site shows a segmented triangle next to a large zigzag (Figure 41). Upon first glance these appear to be separate figures, but upon closer inspection it is apparent that they are actually two different parts of a single rattlesnake figure protruding from different sections of an irregularity in the rock face. On the left, the rattlesnake's rattle projects vertically from a crack in the rock while on the right the snake's body projects from another crack formed by the same irregularity. The rattlesnake's head has been significantly de-emphasized to the point that a very close-up inspection is required to recognize it as such. This goes hand-in-hand with the exaggerated size of the rattle, which the reader might recall, was frequently used by shamans to call Thunder (Spier 1930:119). The remainder of the snake is taken to be hidden within the rock where

Figure 39: The white mineral stain almost perfectly bisects this Columbia Plateau half-and-half spirit figure. Photo by Mike W. Taylor and reproduced with permission.

Figure 40: Prehistoric artists incorporated natural grooves and fissures in the rock face into this red and black depiction of a bison. Reproduced with anonymous owner's permission.

Figure 41: The segmented triangle on the left and zigzag figure on the right are actually two parts of the same "rattlesnake" motif separated by irregularities in the rock face. Photo by Robert David.

it was thought to live. Recalling that every shaman possessed the Rattlesnake Spirit as a medicine (Ray 1963:46), this arrangement very eloquently expresses the concept of shamans' spirit familiars living within the rock and transcending physical and supernatural barriers. The field of drilled holes below this motif indicates that shamans made subsequent visits to consult with this spirit.

     A second example of this kind of interaction is the large sun symbol in section 110N100W (Figure 42). Upon first glance it appears to be an incomplete rayed circle. But a closer look reveals that the two ends that should otherwise be adjoined to form a complete circle near the top instead disappear into the large indentation in the rock face. As before, the suggestion is that the rest of the sun disk is taken to exist within the rock. It is worth recalling that the sun disk symbolized Kumush's medicine. After he created the world, Kumush laid down to sleep beneath The Peninsula, and he sleeps there even today (Marriott and Rachlin 1968:28). In this motif, the artist chose to symbolize this belief not by portraying Kumush himself but instead by portraying his medicine symbol, the sun disk "existing" both inside and outside of the mountain under which he slept.

Figure 42: The missing part of this sun symbol is thought to be hidden inside of the rock face. Photo by MaKai Magié.

     The final example in Figure 43 most directly expresses the ritual philosophy that underlies the creation and use of this site. In this composition, the three anthropomorphic figures from section 110N100W (previously illustrated in Figures 8B–8D) are situated below a large elaborated zigzag. This zigzag figure begins on the left from a pair of cracks in the rock's surface and to the right, each of its peaks disappear into natural cavities in the rock just above. As previously indicated this zigzag figure likely depicts Lightning, the weapon of Yahyahyaas, and here it was clearly intended to draw one's attention. Its deep, sharply defined grooves are made even more visible by its internal elaborations and its prominent position on the rock face. Because of this, it draws one's attention to the anthropomorphic figures associated with it just below. But it is probably no accident that these figures become apparent only with a slight adjustment in one's focus. By way of metaphor, then,

Figure 43: Three anthropomorphic figures situated beneath this elaborated zigzag "canopy" probably denote three spirit beings "illuminated" by Yahyahyaas. Photo by Robert David.

the "illumination" provided by Yahyahyaas (Lightning) made these spirits visible to onlookers. This is highly consistent with the stated explanation for the rock art on this site: shamans visited The Peninsula, under the guidance of Yahyahyaas, to consult with their spirit familiars in matters related to ritual curing. Yahyahyaas was said to have presided over these spirits, indicating that he was the only gateway through which they could be accessed.

The idea that powerful spirits lived within the rocks is certainly consistent with Klamath-Modoc ideology (Marriott and Rachlin 1968:28–29; Spier 1930:100), as well as the ethnography and mythology from adjacent regions (Keyser and Poetschat 2004:125; Whitley 1994:7). Yahyahyaas himself was said to live in the mountains and rocks (Curtin 1912:148), and Spier reported that many mythological beings in Klamath Basin had been transformed to rock by Crow's laughter (Spier 1930:100). Occurrences of rock art–panel face interaction certainly convey this idea, although this is likely not the only explanation for this type of artistic expression. Keyser and Poetschat (2004:121) have also suggested that some of these instances serve as metaphors for shamans' travels to and from the supernatural world, which could be accessed through cracks and fissures in rock faces. In Klamath Basin rock art, both of these explanations seem very likely.

Although power questing has been suggested as a motivation for rock art in this region, neither Klamath nor Modoc ethnography identifies The Peninsula as a place where people would have traveled to in search of supernatural power. It is altogether possible that ethnographic informants either did not recall its importance as a power quest site or purposefully did not report it. This latter explanation is made much more likely given the significant social transformations that were taking place at the time ethnographers were collecting their information in this region. Shamanism was completely outlawed, and all over Agency superintendents and government-backed Christian organizations discouraged the "old ways" (Stern 1966:111). By this time, ethnographic informants may have felt that any information about their Creation point (far removed from the Garden of Eden) was not an important or even safe point to share. Another more likely reason, however, might be that The Peninsula was not thought of as a typical power quest location because its power was restricted to shamans' use. Depictions of so many shamans' spirit familiars certainly support this. If power questing took place at all on The Peninsula, it was very likely done exclusively by shamans.

    Regardless, what is important to remember is that the shaman-artists considered the rock face to be every bit as important as the engravings themselves. Purposefully left untouched, these "blank" spaces on the rock face provided context for the spirit images depicted at other places. In this way, the rock matrix itself served to house these powerful supernatural beings. Vandalism to any part of the rock, regardless of whether or not rock art is present, destroys an important and irreplaceable component of this time-honored spiritual and artistic expression.

Chapter 5

Conclusions

The use of myth in this study is intended to bring Klamath and Modoc voices into research where they have for so long been silent. Crotty was correct when she pointed out that a century of rock art research has systematically excluded the Klamath Basin First People from this important aspect of their heritage (Crotty 1981:167). Elsewhere this exclusionary practice has been called the "colonization of the past" (Atalay 2006:284), and like Crotty, others have begun the tedious task of decolonizing both the practice and interpretation of archaeological phenomenon by including, if not prioritizing, indigenous voices in their research (Atalay 2006:238).

Unfortunately, few Klamath or Modoc today boast any knowledge of their rock art heritage. There are two main reasons for this. The first is simply the fact that, within these groups, rock art was made solely by shamans (Dennison 1879; Gatschet 1890a:179; Spier 1930:142). Although ordinary people certainly would have received occasional insights into particular paintings or glyphs, they did not have the special training necessary to understand them in terms of the wider shamanic practice (Gatschet 1890a:xcviii). The second reason can be attributed to the implementation of various federal assimilation policies in which the practice of shamanism was outlawed on the early Klamath Indian Reservation and replaced with Christianity (Stern 1966:112). Because shamans were the only members of the Klamath-Modoc community to create and utilize rock art, their decline left few qualified people who could discuss it with ethnographers in a meaningful way. Accordingly, the prospect of turning to modern indigenous voices for insight into Klamath Basin rock art seems rather bleak.

We are fortunate, however, for the remarkable Modoc woman Koalakaka who related to Jeremiah and Alma Curtin such an impressive array of sacred narratives in the late nineteenth century. Koalakaka was among the Modoc who were exiled to the Quapaw Agency at the conclusion of the Modoc War of 1872–1873. As a child she was well versed in the myths of her people, having been trained by her grandfather in Modoc religion. Though significantly advanced in age at the time of the Curtins' 1884 visit, she possessed remarkable intelligence and memory (Curtin 1912:vii–viii). Her knowledge of Modoc religion and myths thus makes hers the most ideal voice to guide our understanding of Klamath Basin rock art. It is for that reason I incorporated Klamath-Modoc myth, with an express focus on the materials Koalakaka related to the Curtins, in conjunction with local ethnography as my primary informing resource for this study.

In the past, the use of myth to aid rock art interpretation was avoided based largely on its subjectivity, its inability to accurately explain reality, and of course, the lack of means to reconcile its questionable time-depth with rock art. As we have seen, the petroglyphs at Petroglyph Point have been indirectly dated to between 4500 and 2600 B.P. (Hyder and Lee 1990:200), while the Mod-17 pictographs within Lava Beds National Monument were dated using AMS to A.D. 1020–1290, 1490–1955, and 1440–1670 (Armitage et al. 1997:718). Rau has furthermore indicated that the Klamath were still making rock paintings at the time of his visit to the Klamath Reservation in the late nineteenth century (Rau 1881:65–66). Making rock art in the Klamath Basin has thus been at least a 4,500-year tradition that persisted into historic times.

The narratives Koalakaka provided were contemporaneous with the historically produced rock art. Although there is some support for the notion that the myths have remained intact for an extended period of time, without corresponding evidence the length of time they would have been applicable to the rock art can only be conjectured. Yet debating the longevity of myth is ultimately an unwinnable endeavor, given that both sides of the issue have only ideals and appeals to reason to contribute to the discussion. A more productive use of myth in this kind of research entails setting aside preoccupations with how accurately it represents reality and concentrating instead on the extent to which it reflected and shaped the reality of Klamath-Modoc ancestors who, as a result, produced datable material culture ideologically linked to rock art. By using the direct historical approach, it seems reasonable to take decorated items that are ethnographically associated with shamanism from the recent past and use our modern understanding, derived largely from myth, to form testable hypotheses for dated materials recovered from much older archaeological deposits.

Decorated pipe stems recovered in the Nightfire Island excavation (Figures 44 and 45) show calibrated radiocarbon dates that range from 134 B.C. to A.D. 1000 (Sampson 1985:104, 422). Similarly, Cressman (1956:432, 464) recovered a bird bone bead that exhibited a nucleated circle from his excavation of Kawumkan Springs.[6] This design is found all throughout Klamath Basin rock art and has been widely associated with the mythical character Kumush (David 2005:45; Hann and Bettles 2006:190; Lee et al. 1988:138–139; Whitley et al. 2004:231–233). Other promising items include the decorated flutes in Figure 46 and the medicinal heating stones in Figure 47. Although these items were not recovered from dated archaeological deposits, the decorated flutes were collected from a well-known shaman's site (Curtin 1912:4–5; Howe 1968:209). The heating stones were historically reported to have curative properties, thereby linking them with the shamanic curing practice (Carlson 1959:92). It is possible, and even useful in spite of the lack of good provenience, to radiocarbon date the decorated flutes for comparison with the Nightfire Island pipes that bear similar markings. Moreover, heating stones previously recovered from well-documented archaeological strata may currently be housed within universities and museums that can be used for comparative study, as well as to establish a date range for the designs they bear. By the same token, there will always be times when necessity demands that salvage excavations by cultural resource management firms be conducted where materials of this nature might be recovered from dated archaeological strata. Collecting information in this fashion can assist in establishing a temporal framework with which these design styles may be solidly affiliated. To the extent that the similarities in these designs derived from the same ideology (e.g., myth) that produced the rock art, their persistence through time promises to shed light on how long the ideology itself might have persisted and, by extension, how far through time it expressed a relationship with the rock art.

The study of myth, then, has a strong place in Klamath Basin rock art research. The iconic motifs on this site were identifiable as shamans' medicine spirits only because of the combined information provided by ethnography and myth. While ethnographers like Spier and Ray provided very detailed information about shamans and their spirit helpers, myths collected by Curtin (1884) and others (Barker 1963; Clark 1953; Gatschet 1890; Marriott and Rachlin 1968) described their supernatural abilities—in essence, the very reasons why they made such powerful spirit familiars for shamans.

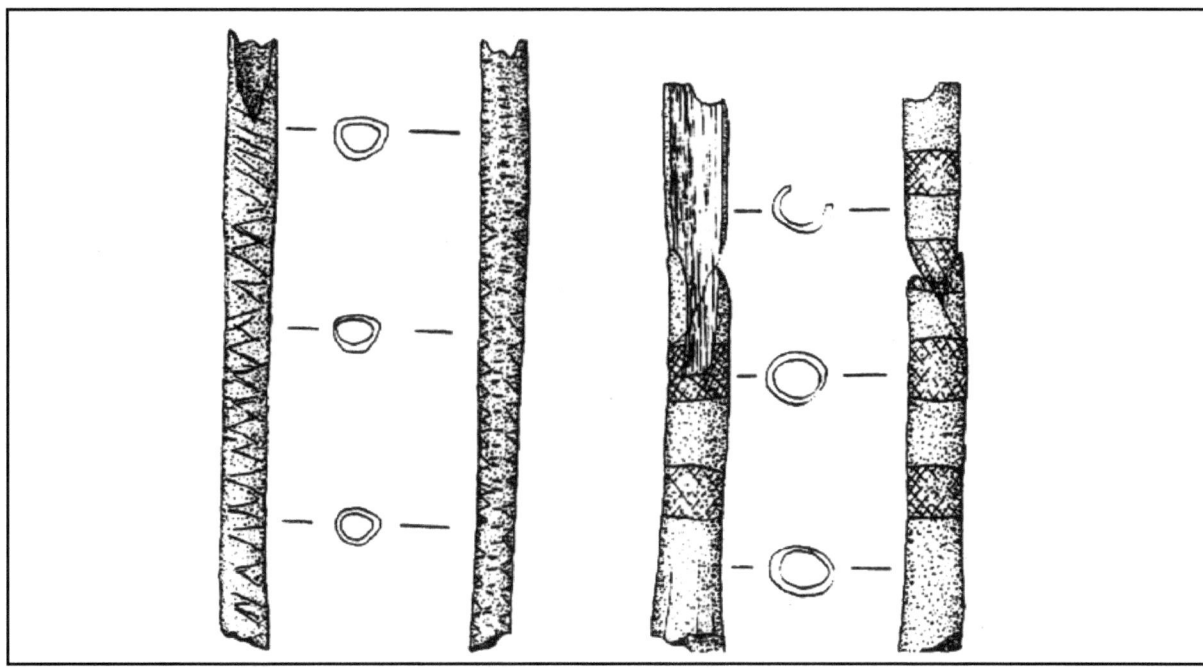

Figure 44: The markings on these pipe mouth pieces from Nightfire Island are similar to Klamath Basin petroglyphs. From Sampson (1985:422:Figure 17-6) and reproduced with permission of the University of Oregon Museum of Natural and Cultural History.

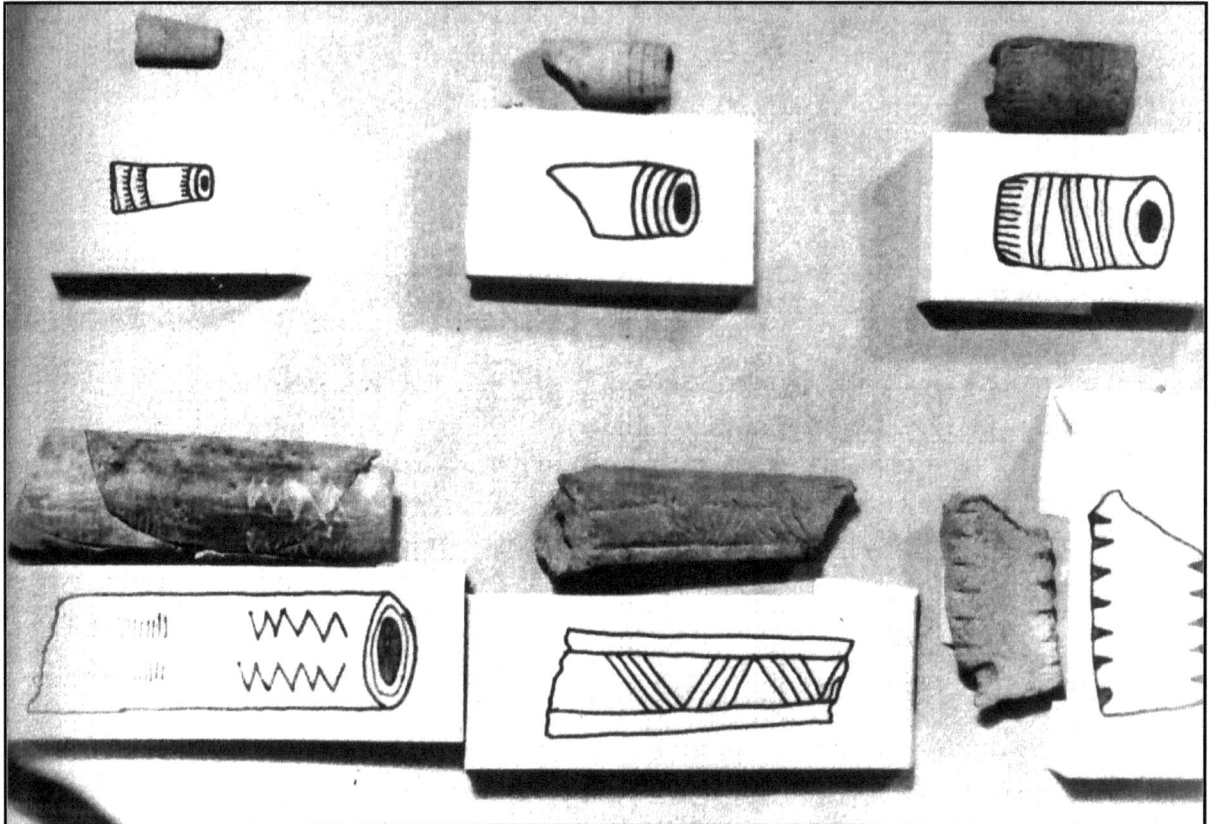

Figure 45: Marked pipe stems from the Nightfire Island excavation date between 13 B.C. and A.D. 1000. Adapted from Howe (1979:135, Figure 122).

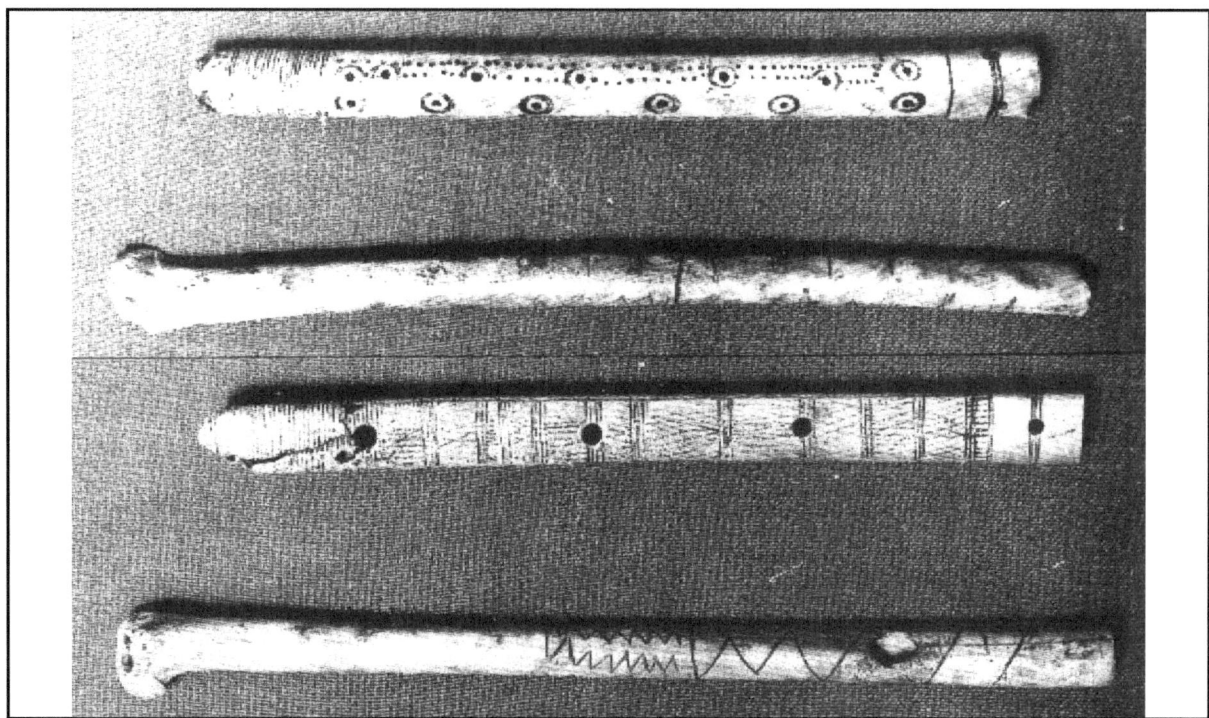

Figure 46: Markings on these bone flutes are very similar to decorated pipes and rock art figures in the Klamath Basin. Adapted from Howe (1968:210: Figure 166).

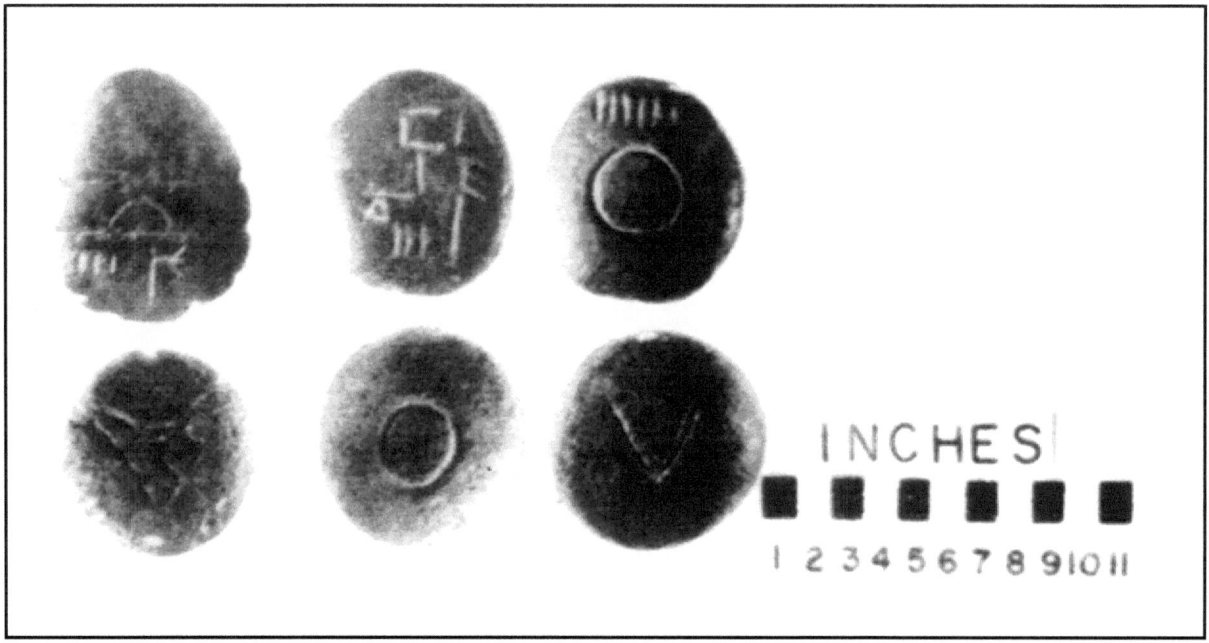

Figure 47: Markings on some of these medicinal heating stones resemble imagery from Petroglyph Point. Reproduced from Carlson (1959:Plate 2).

Similarly, although the myths never explicitly stated that scratching and drilling holes into rocks was necessary to call spirits or to experience visions, the scenarios played out in the stories make it clear that doing these things was a fundamental part of the process. Accordingly, the myths helped to identify the residual markings on 4-Mod-22 (and probably Petroglyph Point) as ritual processes rather than representations of objects or beings. On these grounds we can reject fanciful speculations that they represent a form of ancient Ogham (Kelly 1929), or, as Lee et al. (1988:139) have proposed more recently, that the zigzags represent the Milky Way. While it is likely, based on its importance with so many other surrounding cultures, that the Milky Way was spiritually important to the Klamath and Modoc, there exists no mythological or ethnographic support that would help us link that belief to zigzags and drilled holes. By contrast, the spirit figure Yahyahyaas, and the concept of illumination as expressed by either entoptic phenomena or the spirit Lightning (e.g., zigzags, in either case), are both well supported in Klamath-Modoc ethnography and myth.

The use of myth fosters other advantages as well. As we have seen, it frequently compliments and expands upon statements contained in ethnographic texts, which themselves are often fragmentary and shrouded in cultural metaphors. Spier, for example, insisted that the Klamath did not make pictographs, even though he credited their creation to the mythical being Kemu'kumps (Kumush) and related them to shamanism in the very next sentence (Spier 1930:142). Two of the myths collected by Curtin describe how Kumush marked on the rocks in two locations around Tule Lake, one of which was a smooth cliff face on The Peninsula (Curtin 1884:255; Hann and Bettles 2006:184). The ethnography makes it very clear that mythological characters were the same beings that functioned as shamans' spirit familiars (Gatschet 1890a:c; Spier 1930:103), and furthermore that the behaviors of shamans and their familiars were indistinguishable (Spier 1930:109). Taking this into consideration, it is clear that Spier's informants were speaking from their belief that Kemu'kumps, as a shaman's spirit familiar, had indeed created the rock art, even if those informants had witnessed shamans physically performing the act. From their point of view, Kemu'kumps animated the shamans' hands as he created the art.

In a similar fashion, myth also provides a sense of logic to shamanic ritual that appears otherwise obscure. Elsewhere I have described a ritual in which shamans submerged small stone statuettes called *hen'was* into streams along the banks in order to cure certain types of illness (David 2010:391–393). On the surface, this seems like a rather odd curing rite until one becomes familiar with the corresponding myths. In the tale, Pitoiois (Curtin 1912:318–332), the hen'was belonged to a demented being named Wulkutska, who used it to kill and devour his victims. The hen'was was his medicine. As the story describes, the only way to disenfranchise Wulkutska was to hide his medicine under water along the stream banks. The mythological being Tskel was the only spirit able to accomplish this, which eventually he did and inevitably righted Wulkutska's faulty mind. Tskel, it will be recalled, was a well-established spirit familiar (Gatschet 1890a:ci–cii). It stands to reason that if a shaman diagnosed a sickness among one of the villagers as having been caused by Wulkutska, he or she would have enacted the very cure prescribed in the narrative. At the same time patients would have found great comfort in witnessing the shaman, under the influence of Tskel, disenfranchise Wulkutska by ritually submerging his hen'was in a stream along its bank on their behalf (see David 2010:393). Because the details of the ritual had been encoded in myth, ordinary people who had been exposed to these myths all throughout their lives would have possessed the mental template that effectively made sense of the shamans' ritual actions.

Another advantage to incorporating myth in rock art research is that it associates these stories with sacred places on the landscape (Whitley et al. 2004:227). As previously indicated, Kumush not only created The Peninsula first among all other land masses, he also returned there to "write on the rocks," in preparation for his own power quest (Curtin 1884:255; Marriott and Rachlin 1968:28). In short, myth associated The Peninsula with power questing, Kumush, and the creation of rock art, making The Penninsula an especially powerful monument on the Klamath-Modoc landscape. As a result, shamans embarked on their own power quest rituals around the Basin, and like Kumush, also "wrote" on the rocks at The Peninsula to display their spirits and to commemorate their visionary experiences (Deur 2008:53–54).

Finally, over the course of this study, looking to the myths for insight has led to the realization that ritual actions related to the rock art did not take place exclusively on The Peninsula. As part of their power quest rituals in myth, Kumush and Aisis stacked rocks in the nearby lava fields before approaching the rock art (Curtin 1884:220, 255). Knowing this not only helps us to understand the rock art in terms of a wider ritual context, but also to understand that The Peninsula and lava fields both constituted two interrelated components of a larger ritual arena. Studying either one to the exclusion of the other invariably misses half the point.

To the ancestors of Klamath-Modoc peoples, the spiritual world described in these sacred narratives operated side-by-side with the mundane, physical world. Both of these worlds were simultaneously active, and the people had to be vigilant as they continually negotiated this pluralistic reality. Sacred paraphernalia, such as rock art and marked shamans objects, represented an important interface between these worlds. Whether drawn, painted, scratched, drilled, or pecked, the markings themselves directly appealed to both. In this regard, it seems impossible to understand them in any research endeavor where myth is not consulted.

Nevertheless, the interpretations offered for the 4-Mod-22 petroglyphs are not here considered to be the only possible explanations. Once again, the prioritization of myth was intended to bring a fresh voice into an area of research where it has for so long been absent. Rock art studies in this region will certainly benefit from the continued application of both formal and informed methodologies (Taçon and Chippindale 1998:1–10). The categorical relationships between design styles and rendering techniques identified by Swartz Jr. (1978), and Crotty's reclassification of the rock art categories first proposed by Steward (1929) and continued by Heizer and Clewlow (1973), will provide excellent comparative materials in more formalized studies on 4-Mod-22 that can either support, challenge, or expand upon the results presented here. Only continued research in which a wide variety of models are used can hope to bring us closer to understanding this complex aspect of the Klamath and Modoc people's sacred rock art heritage.

Notes

1. Among the Klamath, Kumush is called Gmok'am'c and is spelled in a number of different ways. Throughout this text, I use both *Kumush* and *Gmok'am'c* wherever culturally or logically appropriate. Moreover, I defer to the spelling *Gmok'am'c*, except where the name is reprinted from other sources and spelled otherwise.

2. Ray refers to this ritual as the "crisis quest" (Ray 1963:31).

3. *Kiuks*, also spelled *qyoqs*, is the Klamath and Modoc term for shaman, or doctor.

4. Spier does not describe how the outfit functions in the curing ritual. However the term *mu'lwas* implies that the outfit was considered part of the shamans' tool kit.

5. In myth, spousal terms are frequently used to describe the relationship between people and their spirit helpers.

6. No image available.

References

Armitage, R. A., M. Hyman, J. Southon, C. Barat, and M. W. Rowe
    1997 Rock Art Image in Fern Cave, Lava Beds National Monument, California: Not the AD 1054 (Crab Nebula) Supernova. *Antiquity* 71:719–721.

Atalay, Sonya
    2006 Indigenous Archaeology as Decolonizing Practice. In *The American Indian Quarterly* 30(3–4):280–310.

Barker, M. A. R.
    1963 *Klamath Texts.* University of California Publications in Linguistics, Vol. 30. University of California Press, Berkeley and Los Angeles.

Blackburn, Thomas C.
    1975 *December's Child: A Book of Chumash Oral Narrative.* University of California Press, Berkeley and Los Angeles.

Carlson, Roy L.
    1959 Klamath Henwas and Other Stone Sculpture. In *American Anthropologist* 61(1):88–96.

Clark, Ella
    1953 *Indian Legends of the Pacific Northwest.* University of California Press, Berkeley and Los Angeles.

Cline, Walter
    1938 Religion and World Views. In *The Sinkaietk or Southern Okanagan of Washington*, edited by L. Spier, pp. 133–182. General Series in Anthropology 6, Contributions from the Laboratory of Anthropology 2. Laboratory of Anthropology, Menasha, Wisconsin.

Coville, Frederick V.
    1897 Notes on the Plants used by the Klamath Indians of Oregon. In *Contributions from the US National Herbarium*, Vol. 5, No. 2, pp. 87–108. Government Printing Office, Washington, D.C.

Cressman, Luther S.
    1956 Klamath Prehistory: The Prehistory of the Culture of the Klamath Lake Area. *Transactions of the American Philosophical Society* 46(4):375–513.

Crotty, Helen K.
    1981 Petroglyph Point Revisited—A Modoc County Site. In *Messages from the Past: Studies in California Rock Art*, edited by Clement W. Meighan, pp. 141–168. UCLA Institute of Archaeology Monograph 20. Regents of University of California, Los Angeles.

Crouch, Carlisle
    1936 *Preliminary Archaeological Reconnaissance, Lava Beds National Monument.* November 18–December 4, 1935. Report housed in Lava Beds New Mexico collection storage facility.

Curtin, Jeremiah
    1884 Miscellaneous Papers and Notes Collected by Jeremiah and Alma Curtin from the Klamath and Modoc Tribes in 1883 and 1884. *Bureau of American Ethnology Documents 1299, 1762,*

2569, 3538, and 3799. Washington, D.C.

1912 *Myths of the Modocs.* Little, Brown, and Company, Boston, Massachusetts.

David, Robert J.
2005 Rock Art as Shamans' Tools: Testing and Refining Landscape Symbolism Models in the Klamath Basin. MA thesis on file at Portland State University, Portland, Oregon.

2010 The Archaeology of Myth: Rock Art, Ritual Objects, and Mythical Landscapes of the Klamath Basin. In *Archaeologies: Journal of the World Archaeological Congress.* 6(2):372–400.

2012a *The Landscape of Klamath Basin Rock Art.* Unpublished Ph.D. dissertation, Department of Anthropology, University of California, Berkeley.

2012b The Holding Hands Petroglyph Site: Using the Ethnographic record and Sacred Space to Illuminate Aspects of a Modoc Rock Art Site. In *American Indian Rock Art,* Vol. 38, edited by Eric W. Ritter, Melissa Greer, and Peggy Whitehead, pp. 53–62. American Rock Art Research Association, Glendale, Arizona.

David, Robert J., and James D. Keyser
2008 A New Ethnographic Reference for Klamath Basin Rock Art: Shamans' Incantations and Sacred Rocks. In *International Newsletter on Rock Art* (INORA), edited by Jean Clottes, 50:26–27.

David, Robert J., and Melissa Morgan
2014 Old Man Owl: Myth and Gambling Medicine in Klamath Basin Rock Art. In *Rock Art and Sacred Landscapes,* edited by Donna L. Gillette, Mavis Greer, Michele Helene Hayward, and William Breen Murray, pp. 163–176. Springer, New York.

Dennison, J. S.
1879 Unpublished Letters to Albert Gatschet. *Bureau of American Ethnology* document No. 315. Smithsonian Institution, Washington, D.C.

Deur, Douglass
2008 *In the Footprints of Gmukamps: A Traditional Use Study of Crater Lake National Park and Lava Beds National Monument.* National Park Service, Pacific West Region.

Devereux, George
1949 Magic Substances and Narcotics of the Mohave Indians. *British Journal of Medical Psychology* 22:110–116.

Donnelly-Nolan, Julie. M., and Duane E. Champion
1987 Geologic Map of Lava Beds National Monument, Northern California. USGS Map 1-1804.

Echo-Hawk, Roger
2000 Ancient History in the New World: Integrating Oral Traditions and the Archaeological Record in Deep Time. *American Antiquity,* 65(2):267–290.

Eichmeier, Joseph, and Oskar Höfer
1974 *Endogene Bildmuster.* Munich, Urban and Schwarzenberg.

Eliade, Mircea
1964 *Shamanism: Archaic Techniques of Ecstasy.* Princeton University Press, Princeton, New Jersey.

Fitzgerald, Richard, T.
  1992 Petroglyph Point Archaeological Survey of 1992, Lava Beds National Monument, Modoc County, California. Report on file at the National Park Service, Arcata, California.

Gates, Gerald R.
  1982 Tule Lake National Wildlife Refuge Land Exchange: Archaeological Reconnaissance Report ARR 05-9-17 (CY-82). On file, Klamath Basin National Wildlife Refuges, Tulelake, California.

Gatschet, Albert S.
  1890a The Klamath Indians of Southwestern Oregon. Contributions to North American Ethnology, Vol. 1. U.S. Geologic and Geological Survey of the Rocky Mountain Region, Contributions to North American Ethnology. Washington D.C. Government Printing Office.

  1890b *The Klamath Indians of Southwestern Oregon. Contributions to North American Ethnology*, Vol. 2. U.S. Geologic and Geological Survey of the Rocky Mountain Region, Contributions to North American Ethnology. Washington D.C. Government Printing Office.

Gayton, Anna H.
  1948 Yokuts and Western Mono Ethnography. *University of California Anthropological Records* 10:1–290.

Gayton, Anna H., and Stanley S. Newman
  1940 Yokuts and Western Mono Myths. *University of California Anthropological Records* 5:1–110. Berkeley.

Gifford, Edward W.
  1932 The Northfork Mono. *University of California Publications in American Archaeology and Ethnography* 31(2):15–65.

Grant, Campbell
  1967 *Rock Art of the American Indian*. Promontory Press, New York.

Hann, Donald T.
  2012 Implied Narrative: Rock Art, Landscape, and Myth at Picture Gorge, Oregon. *American Indian Rock Art*, Vol. 39, edited by William D. Hyder, pp. 101–113. American Rock Art Research Association, Glendale, Arizona.

Hann, Donald T., and Gordon Bettles
  2006 House of the Rising Sun: Using the Ethnographic Record to Illuminate Aspects of Klamath Basin Rock Art. In *Talking with the Past: The Ethnography of Rock Art*, edited by James D. Keyser, George Poetschat, and Michael W. Taylor, pp. 176–199. Oregon Archaeological Society, Portland.

Hann, Don, James D. Keyser, and P. Cash Cash
  2010 Columbia Plateau Rock Art: A Window to the Spirit World. In *Rock Art of the Oregon Country: Honoring the Lorings' Legacy*, edited by James D. Keyser and George Poetschat, pp. 1–24. Oregon Archaeological Society, Portland.

Heinze, Ruth-Inge
  1986 More on Mental Imagery and Shamanism. *Current Anthropology* 27(2):154.

Heizer, R. F., and M. A. Baumhoff
  1962 *Prehistoric Rock Art of Nevada and Eastern California.* University of California Press, Berkeley and Los Angeles.

Heizer, Robert F., and C. William. Clewlow Jr.
  1973 Prehistoric Rock Art of California. Ballena Press, Socorro.

Hill-Tout, Charles
  1978 *The Salish People: The Local Contribution of Charles Hill-Tout, Vol. 1, The Thompson and Okanagan,* edited with an introduction by Ralph Maud. Talonbooks, Vancouver.

Horowitz, M. J.
  1964 The Imagery of Visual Hallucinations. *Journal of Nervous and Mental Disease.* 138:513–523.

  1975 Hallucinations: An Information Processing Approach. In *Hallucinations: Behaviour, Experience, and Theory,* edited by R. K. Siegel and L. J. West, pp. 163–195. Wiley, New York.

Horton, Robin
  1982 Tradition and Modernity Revisited. In *Rationality and Relativism,* edited by M. Hollis and S. Lukes, pp. 201–260. The MIT Press, Cambridge, Massachusetts.

Howe, Carroll B.
  1968 *Ancient Tribes of the Klamath Country.* Binford and Mort, Portland, Oregon.

  1979 *Ancient Modocs of California and Oregon.* Binford and Mort, Portland, Oregon.

Jensen, Peter M., and Alfred Farber
  1982 Archaeological Data Recovery at CA-SIS-342 on 02-SIS-97, P.M. 41.5 to 42.3, Department of Transportation, Redding, California. Report submitted to California Department of Transportation, Sacramento.

Kelly, John W.
  1929 Mystery of the Klamath Basin. *Portland Oregonian.* November 10.

Keyser, James D.
  1992 *Indian Rock Art of the Columbia Plateau.* University of Washington Press, Seattle and London.

Keyser, James D., and George Poetschat
  2004 The Canvas as the Art: Landscape Analysis of the Rock Art Panel. In *The Figured Landscapes of Rock art: Looking at Pictures in Place,* edited by Christopher Chippindale and George Nash, pp. 118–130. University of Cambridge Press, New York.

Keyser, James D., G. Poetschat, H. Hiczun, P. McCoy, and B. Tandberg
  2006 The Beaver Bowl: Ethnographic Evidence for a Northwest Coast Shaman's Petroglyph. In *Talking with the Past: The Ethnography of Rock Art,* edited by James D. Keyser, George Poetschat, and Michael W. Taylor, pp. 158–175. Oregon Archaeological Society, Portland.

Keyser, James D., and Michael W. Taylor
  2002 *Visions on Stone: Rock Art of the Columbia Plateau.* Oregon Archaeological Society, Portland.

  2006 The Blade Cuts Two Ways: Using Ethnographic Analogy to Interpret the Columbia

Plateau Scratched Style. In *Talking with the Past: The Ethnography of Rock Art*, edited by James D. Keyser, George Poetschat, and Michael W. Taylor, pp. 200–224. Oregon Archaeological Society, Portland.

Keyser, James D, Michael W. Taylor, and George R. Poetschat
2004 *Echoes of the Ancients: Rock Art of The Dalles-Deschutes Region.* Oregon Archaeological Society, Portland.

Knoll, Max
1958 Anregung geometrischer Figuren und anderer subjektiver Lichtmuster in elektrischen Feldern. *Zeitschrift für Psychologie* 17:110–126.

Kroeber, Alfred L.
1907a The Yokuts Language of South-Central California. *University of California Publications in American Archaeology and Ethnology* 2(5):165–378. Berkeley.

1907b The Religion of the Indians of California. *University of California Publications in American Archaeology and Ethnology* 4(6):319–369. Berkeley.

La Barre, Weston
1980 *Culture in Context.* Duke University Press, Durham, North Carolina.

Laird, Carobeth
1975 *Encounter with an Angry God: Recollections of my life with John Peabody Harrington.* Malki Museum, Banning.

1976 *The Chemehuevis.* Malki Museum, Banning.

1984 *Mirror and Pattern: George Laird's World of Chemehuevi Mythology.* Malki Museum, Banning.

Lee, Georgia, and William. D. Hyder
1990 Prehistoric Rock Art as an Indicator of Cultural Interaction and Tribal Boundaries in South-Central California. *Journal of California and Great Basin Anthropology* 13:15–28.

Lee, Georgia, William. D. Hyder, and Arlene Benson
1988 The Rock Art of Petroglyph Point and Fern Cave, Lava Beds National Monument. Unpublished Manuscript, Lava Beds National Monument, Tulelake, California.

Lewis-Williams, J. D.
2001 Brainstorming Images: Neuropsychology and Rock Art Research. In *Handbook of Rock Art Research*, edited by David S. Whitley, pp. 332–357. AltaMira Press, New York.

2002 The Mind in the Cave: Consciousness and the Origins of Art. Thames and Hudson Ltd. London.

Lewis-Williams, J. D., and T. A. Dowson
1988 The Signs of all Times: Entopic Phenomena in Upper Paleolithic Art. In *Current Anthropology* 29:201–245.

Lorenz, Claudia S.
1969 *The Time of my Life.* Klamath County Museum Research Papers No. 4. Klamath County Museum, Klamath Falls, Oregon.

Loring, Malcolm J., and Louise Loring
    1983 *Pictographs and Petroglyphs of the Oregon Country, Part II: Southern Oregon.* Monograph No. 33. Institute of Archaeology, University of California, Los Angeles.

Loubser, Johannes J., and David S. Whitley
    1999 Recording Eight Places with Rock Art Imagery: Lava Beds National Monument Northern California. 3 vols. Report on File Lava Beds National Monument, Tulelake, California.

Lowie, Robert H.
    1909 The Northern Shoshone. *Anthropological Papers of the American Museum of Natural History* 2(2):165–306.

Marriott, Alice, and Carol K. Rachlin
    1968 *American Indian Mythology*. Thomas Y. Crowell Company, New York.

Mason, Roland
    2000 Archaeology and Native North American Oral Traditions. *American Antiquity* 65(2):239–266.

Myers, L. Daniel
    1987 *Levels of Context: A Sombolic Analysis of Numic Origin Myths*. PhD dissertation, Department of Anthropology, Rutgers University, University Microfilms, Ann Arbor.

New Horizon Technologies, Inc.
    1998 Integrated Pest Management Plan for Leased Lands at Lower Klamath and Tule Lake Natural Wildlife Refuges Oregon/California. Prepared for Bureau of Reclamation, Klamath Basin Area Office, Klamath Falls, Oregon.

Pendergast, David M., and Clement W. Meighan
    1959 Folk Traditions as Historical Facts: A Paiute Example. *Journal of American Folklore* 72:128–133.

Poetschat, George, James D. Keyser, and Johannes H. N. Loubser
    2010 The Mill Creek Sites, Fremont National Forest, Lakeview, Oregon. In *Rock Art of the Oregon Country: Honoring the Lorings' Legacy*, edited by James Keyser and George Poetschat, pp. 93–107. Oregon Archaeological Society, Portland.

Raglan, Fitz R. S. S. (Lord)
    1960 Folk Traditions as Historical Facts. *Journal of American Folklore* 73:58–59.

Rau, Charles
    1881 Observations on Cup-shaped and other Lapidarian Sculptures in the Old World and America. Contributions to North American Ethnology, U.S. Geographical and Geological Survey of the Rocky Mountain Region, Washington.

Ray, Verne F.
    1963 Primitive Pragmatists: The Modoc Indians of Northern California. University of Washington Press, Seattle.

Richards, Whitman
    1971 The Fortification Illusions of Migraines. *Scientific American* 224:89–94.

Riddle, Jeff
  1890 *Unpublished letters to Albert Gatschet.* Bureau of American Ethnology, Document No. 3743 on file at Smithsonian Institution, Washington D.C.

Ritter, Eric W.
  1999 Boundary, Style and Function: Extrapolations from the Keno, Oregon Pictographs. In *American Indian rock Art*, Vol. 25, edited by Steven m. Freers, pp. 81–100. American Rock Art research Association. San Miguel, California.

Sampson, Garth
  1985 Nightfire Island: Later Holocene Lake Marsh Adaptation on the Western Edge of the Great Basin. *University of Oregon Anthropological Papers* 33, Eugene, Oregon.

Siegel, Ronald K., and Murray E. Jarvik
  1975 Drug-induced Hallucinations in Animals and Man. In *Hallucinations: Behavior Experience, and Theory*, edited by R. K. Siegel and L. J. West, pp. 81–161. Wiley, New York.

Spier, Leslie
  1930 Klamath Ethnography. University of California Publications in American Archaeology and Ethnography 30(1):1–338.

Stern, Theodore
  1966 The Klamath Tribe: A People and Their Reservation. University of Washington Press, Seattle.

Sterns, Harold T.
  1928 Lava Beds National Monument, California. *Geological Society of Philadelphia, Bulletin* 26(4):238–253.

Stone, Eric
  1932 *Medicine among the American Indian.* Paul B. Hoeber, Inc., New York.

Swartz, B. K., Jr.
  1978 *Klamath Basin Petroglyphs.* Revised and Abridged. Ballena Press Anthropological Papers No. 12. Ballena Press, New Mexico.

  1998 A Comparative Design Element Analysis of Klamath Basin (Modoc), Southern Sierra (Yokuts), and Santa Barbara (Chumash) Pictograph Styles, California-Oregon. In *Rock Art Studies in the Great Basin*, edited by Eric Ritter, pp. 113–124. Archives of Great Basin Prehistory, No. 1. Coyote Press, Salinas, California.

  2006 Minimum Recording Standards Proposed by the American Committee to Advance the Study of Petroglyphs and Pictographs. In *Rock Art Research* 23(2):264–265.

Taçon, Paul S. C., and Christopher Chippindale
  1998 An archaeology of Rock Art through Informed Methods and Formal Methods. In *The Archaeology of Rock Art*, edited by Christopher Chippindale and Paul S. C. Taçon, pp. 1–10. Cambridge University Press, New York.

Teit, James
  1896 A Rock Painting of the Thompson River Indians. *American Museum of Natural History Bulletin* 8:227–230.

1906 The Lillooet Indians. Memoirs of the American Museum of Natural History 2(5):193–300.

1909 The Shushwap. Memoirs of the American Museum of Natural History 2(8):443–789.

1918 Notes on Rock Paintings in General, 1918. Unpublished manuscript, Alberta, Institute Archives, Glenbow.

1930 The Salishan Tribes of the Western Plateau. In *Bureau of American Ethnology 45th Annual Report*. Smithsonian Institution, Washington, D.C.

Thrall Rogers, Barbara, and Anna H. Gayton
1944 Twenty-Seven Chukchansi Yokuts Myths. *Journal of American Folklore* 57(225):190–207.

Tyler, Christopher. W.
1978 Some New Entoptic Phenomena. *Vision Research* 18:1633–1639.

Wainwright, Ian N. M.
1990 Rock Painting and Petroglyph Recording Projects in Canada. In Cultural Resource Recording *APT Bulletin* 22(1–2):55–79.

Whitley, David S.
1982 Notes on the Coso Petroglyphs, the Etiological Mythology of the Western Shoshone, and the Interpretation of Rock Art. *Journal of California and Great Basin Anthropology* 4:262–271.

1994 Shamanism, Natural Modeling and the Rock Art of far Western North American Hunter-Gatherers. In *Shamanism and Rock Art in North America*, edited by Solveig A. Turpin, pp. 1–44. Rock Art Foundation Special Publication 1. San Antonio, Texas.

1998 Finding Rain in the Desert: Landscape, Gender and far Western North American Rock Art. In *The Archaeology of Rock Art*, edited by Christopher Chippindale and Paul S. Tacon, pp. 15–29. Cambridge University Press, New York.

2000 *The Art of the Shaman: Rock Art of California*. University of Utah Press, Salt Lake City.

Whitley, David S., Johannes H. N. Loubser, and Don Hann
2004 Friends in Low Places: Rock Art and Landscape on the Modoc Plateau. In *The Figured Landscapes of Rock Art: Looking at Pictures in Place*, edited by Christopher Chippindale and George Nash, pp. 217–238. University of Cambridge Press, New York.

Winter, Joseph C.
2000 *Tobacco Use by Native North Americans: Sacred Smoke and Silent Killer*. Civilizations of the American Indian Series, University of Oklahoma Press, Norman.

York, Annie, Richard. Daly, and Chris. Arnett
1993 *They Write their Dreams on Rocks Forever: Rock Writings of the Stein River Valley of British Columbia*. Talonbooks, Vancouver, B.C.

Younger, Janice
1974 Archaeological Site Survey Record, Big Bend Petroglyphs (CA-Sha-661).

1980 Kawaiisu Mythology: An Oral Tradition of South-Central California. Ballena Press, Socorro.

INDEX

A
Aisis, 46, 53–54, 56, 74
altered states of consciousness, 1, 5, 9, 46, 50, 56, 59–60
animal spirits, 14, 43
anthropomorphic, 26–28, 31, 38, 46–47, 58, 62, 65, 66

B
barred rectangle, 40, 59–60
bisected diamonds, 38, 57

C
Captain Jack's Cave, 4
chronometric dating, 8
consultations, shamans/shamanic, 16, 43–44, 46, 48–49, 55, 60
Crater Lake, 22–24
crow (Crow's laughter), 61, 66
cupules, 33, 41, 51–52, 55
Curly Headed Doctor, 4

D
death, symbolic, 59
distance killing, 4
drilled holes, 25, 31–36, 47–50, 54–55, 65, 73

E
enhanced natural features, 60
entoptic, 5, 19–24, 25, 56, 59–60, 73

F
fire drill, 25, 34, 55
flute, 70, 72

G
gashing, ritual, 51
geometric forms/figures/motifs/shapes, 19–21, 25–26, 31, 36, 37, 40–41, 44, 51, 56, 59
ghost Dance, 4
Gmok'am'c (see also Kumush), 4, 6–7

H
head scratchers, 53–54
heating stones, medicinal, 70, 72
hen'was, 73

I
iconic hallucinations/figures/images/motifs, 19, 21, 25–26, 31, 33, 36, 40–41, 44, 50–51, 53–50, 60, 70
incantations, 1, 49
indirect dating, 7–8
inversion, symbolic, 6, 54–55

K
Kiuks, 14, 43
Koalakaka, 69–70
Kumush, 3, 16, 22, 43–46, 50, 53–56, 60, 65–66, 70, 73–74, 75

L
land of the dead, 45
lava, beds: 3–8, 26, 38, 41, 43, 57–58, 70
    lava fields, 46, 50, 53, 56, 74
lightning, 21, 29, 53, 56, 65, 66, 73
lines, scratched/engraved, 32, 33, 50, 54
Lulusdewieas, 4, 46

M
medicine: 44–45, 47, 50, 65, 73
    disk, 3
    stick, 32, 49
    symbol, 45, 65
    pole, 4
    pipe, 4
    man, 4, 24
    outfit, 16
    spirit, 49, 70
Modoc War, 4, 69
Morning Star, 44–45
Mt. Shasta, 14, 23
Mu'lwas, 16, 75
mythological beings, 6, 15, 43, 59, 66

N

neuropsychological model, 1, 5, 9, 19–22

O

ovoid chains, 38, 57 (see also bisected diamond)

P

panel face interaction, 62, 66
Peninsula, The, 1–4, 9, 11–12, 16, 22, 32–34, 41, 43, 44, 46, 50, 54, 59–660, 62, 65, 66–67, 73–74
Petroglyph Point, 1–6, 8–9, 11–12, 18, 26–29, 31, 33, 36–40, 43, 50, 53, 58–59, 69, 72–74
pine marten, 32, 49
pipe, decorated stems, 70, 72
Pitoiois, 73
power:
    song, 3, 5
    quest, 3, 7, 13–15, 19, 43–44, 46, 50, 53–56, 58, 60, 66, 67
Psaudiwas, 46–47, 61

R

rain rocks, 52
rattlesnake, spirit, 26, 30–31, 33, 37, 40–41, 47–49, 65–66
residual markings, 25, 31, 35, 41, 44, 47, 50, 54, 56–57, 73

S

shaman: 2–4, 6–7, 14–16, 19–20, 22–23, 24, 27, 36, 41, 43–51, 53–61, 63, 65, 67–70, 72–74
    initiates, 5, 13–15, 24
    tools/objects, 74
    practice, 1, 22, 69–70
    ritual, 1, 9, 45, 73–74
    winter performance, 7, 22
Skoks, 22, 45, 58, 60, 61
Smoking, ritual, 1, 4, 56, 58
sorcery, 4, 49
spirit: 4, 7, 13–16, 22, 24, 26, 32, 43–51
    helper-familiar, 5, 14–16, 22, 36, 43–47, 49–50, 53–56, 63
    abode(s)/dwelling(s)/locale(s), 43, 55, 59
    consultations, 43–44, 46, 48, 61
    figure, 28–29, 47–48, 53, 62–63, 73
    power, 14
    quest, 5, 15–16, 54
    world/land, 3, 6, 45, 55–59, 61–63, 72–74
stacked rock features/rock cairns, 3, 54, 74
sun disk, 44–45, 65
supernatural: 47, 60, 62, 65
    abilities/potency/power, 1–4, 6–7, 12, 15, 19, 23–24, 43–44, 46–47, 51–52
    assistance, 3, 44
    being(s), 46, 62, 68
    events, 22
    treatments, 15
    universe/world, 1–2, 4–6, 16, 20, 43–44, 47, 52–57, 60, 68
sweat lodge, 44, 54

T

Thunder, Spirit, 14, 43, 45, 47–48, 53, 62
tobacco, native, 3, 49–50, 53, 56–59
trance: 2–6, 8–9, 19–22, 27, 44–50, 55, 56–61
    Imagery, 1, 5–6
Tskel, 32, 49–50, 73
Tule Lake, 1, 4, 8, 11–12, 34, 41, 50, 53–54, 73

V

Venus, 44
vision quest, shamanic (see power/spirit quest)

W

wavy lines, 25, 30, 56
Wulkutska, 22, 73

Y

Yahyahyaas, 22, 44, 47–48, 50, 53, 55, 58, 62, 65–66, 73
Yaulilik, daughters, 53–54

Z

zigzag: 19–21, 25, 27, 29–34, 36–39, 50, 53–56, 59, 62, 64–66, 73
    paired, 32, 36, 37, 53, 56, 59
    concentrations, 53, 56

About the Author

Dr. Robert David is a Klamath Tribal member who grew up in Chiloquin, Oregon, the main town on the former Klamath Indian Reservation. A graduate of anthropology from University of California, Berkeley, he has studied his own tribe's rock art since 1999. In addition to his dissertation and various technical reports on rock art for government land management agencies, he has also written several research papers for publication. He currently lives in Berkeley, California, where he works as a self-employed archaeological contractor and occasionally teaches classes on various subjects at the university.

www.ingramcontent.com/pod-product-compliance
Lightning Source LLC
Chambersburg PA
CBHW041515220426
43668CB00002B/30